Alameda Free Library - City

ALAMEDA—Spanish word for grove of poplars
or shaded walk; mall.

a gift honoring the memory of

ANITA KELEHER

donated by

DONALD J. KELEHER

I Want to Thank My Brain for Remembering Me

Also by Jimmy Breslin
in Large Print:

Table Money

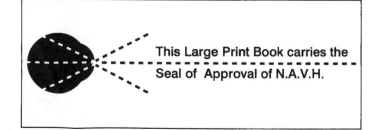

This Large Print Book carries the
Seal of Approval of N.A.V.H.

I Want to Thank My Brain for Remembering Me

Jimmy Breslin

Thorndike Press • Thorndike, Maine

Copyright © 1996 by Jimmy Breslin

Published in 1997 by arrangement with Little Brown and Co., Inc.

Thorndike Large Print ® Americana Series.

The tree indicium is a trademark of Thorndike Press.

The text of this Large Print edition is unabridged.
Other aspects of the book may vary from the original edition.

Set in 16 pt. Plantin.

Printed in the United States on permanent paper.

Library of Congress Cataloging in Publication Data

Breslin, Jimmy.
    I want to thank my brain for remembering me : a
memoir / Jimmy Breslin.
      p.   cm.
    ISBN 0-7862-0971-2 (lg. print : hc)
    1. Breslin, Jimmy. 2. Journalists — New York —
Biography. I. Title.
[PN4874.B67A3   1997]
070'.92—dc21
[B]   96-49644

For Deirdre Breslin

1

It is morning in Phoenix, Arizona, and the nurse walks in and I am awake. I don't even remember going to sleep.

"How are you?"

"I could use some coffee," I said.

"You can't have anything," she said.

"Come on, I can have coffee."

"You can't have anything if you're having brain surgery," she said.

She handed me these long surgical stockings. They are supposed to help keep your blood vessels intact from head to toe. I was tugging them on when my wife and daughter walked in. I was so calm that my daughter thought I had been given a lot of Valium. And I had nothing yet. The hand of God kept the fear out of me.

"What's in the papers?" I said.

They looked at me.

"That's all right. I'm the big news today. You could ask the Bo Gee. Did I ever tell you about him?"

"A thousand times," my wife said. I told

them, anyway. The Bo Gee was a little man who pulled a cart of Chinese-language newspapers that he sold in the kitchens of Chinese restaurants on the East Side. He walked in holding out the papers and bawling, "Bon suy." Pay me! They gave him a drink in every place he went into. There are a thousand Chinese restaurants on the East Side and he took a thousand drinks. Usually he never got to the last restaurants, up in the 80s and 90s. The waiters were lucky to get week-old news of Canton.

At the bar, the Bo Gee always called out the two biggest-selling news stories. Which I repeated here in the hospital room:

"War!"

"Big Guy Dies."

"It's all right if I go out of the picture today," I said to Ronnie Eldridge, my wife. "I'm in the state of Grace. I can go. You ever think of that?"

"Why do you think I have so much anxiety today?" she said.

"What are you, afraid of losing your second husband in a row? That you have to put on another black dress?" I asked.

"I don't wear black to funerals," she said. "Navy blue." She walked to the closet to get my clothes. After the operation, I was not going to be brought back to this room.

"I wore yellow to Robert Kennedy's. Everybody saw me on television."

I asked her, "I'm serious. I could go out of the picture. Has that occurred to you?"

"I'm well aware of what can happen. Especially because they didn't take my other husband seriously."

"That's why you're over my shoulder every time we see a doctor," I said.

"He had a pain in his chest. The general practitioner told him that he should play squash. His psychiatrist told him it was from anxiety."

She said no more. But I remembered how she had told me about that October night when her husband came home in a cab, sitting in the far corner so the small light on the side would let him see the newspaper. She said he had to be busy and couldn't wait to read it at home. He told her that he didn't feel well when he got into the house and he went upstairs. She checked him once and called the doctor. He was away and his answering service said they must have cash if a covering doctor was sent. Ronnie said she had a check. The answering service operator said that, oh, we need cash; you have no idea of how many bad checks people give us. She found another doctor who came and urged him to go to the hospital but he refused. He went to sleep. Later, she went upstairs to check him and found him obviously stricken in the bathroom. She helped him back to the bedroom and put him on the bed and he died. Just like that. She called the service again. Then she sat on the iron staircase in the back of the house and waited for the dawn when she had to tell her three children, with their big wide eyes, that their father was dead.

When she told me this, she did it in only a couple of sentences and a calm voice, but one of such intensity that the picture stayed in my mind until this moment.

Just as I suddenly saw the late night when I walked under the dripping trees and into the house and woke up my youngest boy, Christopher, to tell him that his mother, Rosemary, my first wife, had just died. He thrashed upright, then shook his head. "I just need a minute." He sat there with his head down. He shook it. Then he stood up. "All right."

Two families, with all the smiles and laughter and hands held and dreams dreamed, suddenly maimed by death, and then the woman and man coming upon each other and starting off on another path. And now this happens to me.

10

Here is my daughter, Rosemary, thirty-eight and beautiful. She spent a year sitting on the bed and doing crossword puzzles with her sick mother. She has spent the last seven years with a rare blood disease. An antibody attacks her red blood cells before they mature. She goes to Memorial Sloan-Kettering hospital every seventeen days for an infusion of gamma globulin. I go to visit her, I'm so nervous I can't control myself. Once, four veins had blown before they found one in her hand that could hold a needle. I came in with cappuccino and held it out to her. Here, here, something good. I bumped into the IV pole or the table next to it, I don't know, and I pitched forward and caused the needle to come out of her vein. Coffee spilled all over her expensive pants. "I can't take any more of this," I said. Yes, I could. I did it a few times.

Now she is a nervous young woman tapping, shifting, touching, her eyes bleak. I am in bed without a yawn in me.

The priest came in. "I want to receive communion," I said.

"They don't allow it," he said. "The wafer is too thick. They don't want anything in you."

He suggested that we say a prayer. So my daughter, wife and I and the priest held

11

hands in a circle and he said the Our Father and I don't know what other prayer was recited, if any. I concentrated on my Act of Contrition again. But we were in this tight circle, a huddle, and I thought of these college teams in a huddle praying to God before they ran out onto the field. What the hell is that all about? Praying for a first down? What kind of a value is this? Young primitives with their eyes closed, not even knowing the words of a prayer; they hardly know their own names; grasping coaches asking God to get them a Nike contract. A fighter blesses himself in the corner. Will it help? Yes. If he can punch.

Then the priest left and the three of us stood in the room and looked around for anything, staying busy on something small to kill time while waiting for something big to start. Tricks I'd seen in other places, the prizefighter staying busy putting new laces in his shoes, going to the bathroom in case, an actor rehearsing lines. But there was nothing to do. Just a bare room and a stillness of waiting.

From the hallway came the sound of metal rattling and wheels groaning and squeaking loudly. Suddenly in the doorway here was the nurse, and an attendant who pushed a gurney right into the room.

"You ready?" she said.

"I guess so."

"Then we'll go."

"I can walk," I said.

"No, you can't," the nurse said.

I had to get on the gurney.

"All right," the attendant said.

"Yep."

"All right then."

The nurse went first. She had her hand on the side of the gurney and the attendant pushed from the back and my wife and daughter were with him and we went down one hall and on to another and we all went towards the operating room where I was going to have a brain operation.

We were still in a hallway someplace and the nurse said to my wife and daughter that they had to leave us now. There was a waiting room right there, she said. The two of them kissed me.

"Don't worry, I'm in the state of Grace if I go."

I meant it as a half smart remark and also as a statement of fact and maybe it killed them. My daughter was more worried about me coming out frothing at the mouth for the rest of my life.

The state of Grace lifted just enough for me to experience a little anxiety about something happening to the front of my brain, where any ability to write begins. The young guy back in the room alongside mine had received a blow on the head and for some time had been unable to use nouns.

We had made a point of not mentioning it, and Ronnie and Rosemary were distressed because I knew about it. How did they expect me not to know about it, when one of his family was standing in the hallway and tapping the door and saying:

"What is this?"

"A . . . taxicab," the young guy called out.

Later, I heard the same guy in the doorway. "What is this?" I guess he was holding something up.

"Taxicab," the young guy in bed said.

And it might be a taxicab forever. That, and almost every other object you pointed to.

I knew that if something happened to the curl in my brain that causes verbs, I would be one of those home relief cases that people hate so much.

They began wheeling me again and my wife and daughter were gone and I sure didn't want to start thinking about not being able to write a verb: rush, race, run, gallop, canter, veer, saunter. What if they all came out as "bus"? Right away, I stopped that thought. Then right away I thought, Imagine if I lose the ability to stop thoughts. A thing just like this, about not knowing verbs, would be in my mind all day. It would just hang there like a sign painted on a building wall. I wouldn't be able to peel it off. I would be stark mad by four each day. I thought about the Orwell short story where the guy going to the gallows walks around a puddle of water. Maybe there was something that small around me now that I could concentrate on. But the cart is running so fast that the ceiling tiles are flying too fast for me. I can't fix my eyes on anything. So I say the hell with it and I can't understand why I am not so frozen with fear that my mind won't work, and I don't want to think about that. Who knows, I'll start falling apart and crying like Cagney did in the big electrocution scene in *Angels with Dirty Faces*. Oh, of course I thought of that. More middle-aged people going for an operation see that Cagney scene than anything else.

I concentrated on beauty. The painting of the ocean that Eddie Weisl had in his apartment in the Hampshire House. I used to go there to sit and dream. From nowhere, I wonder what happened to the Rubens painting the old lady had.

She was a wonderful old woman. I met her in the rain in London when I was sent hurriedly to write about Winston Churchill, who was dying. It was the first time I ever was east of Rockaway Beach. I arrived in a Saturday morning rain, with no passport or clothes. I walked straight through customs and went right to Churchill's house, a big red brick house on a street called Hyde Park Gate. Look at this. Thirty-one years later and I remember the street name.

I had been intimidated by this crowd of British reporters on the street, their precise speech so wondrous, as a contrast to my Myrtle Avenue voice, their expensive trench coats showing up my wet, wrinkled overcoat. Then I saw the woman come down that street like Great Britain. Her head was held higher than a lion's and the cane hooked over her arm was there for any emergency. The instant I saw her, I walked right after her. All my insecurity dissolved when I saw that the rest of them didn't have the sense to go after her. I knew what I needed to make a living and she was a column sent from the sky. She had on a blue hat with an enormous bow on its front. She had it clamped to her hair by a stick-pin. Her form-fitting brown coat came to her calves, the matching skirt fluttering at

16

her ankles. She walked in laced low-heel shoes like a bird-watcher stomping through woods. She was eighty and she was going to visit Winston Churchill in the brick house at the end of the street. Her name was Lady Helen Cynthia Colville, and she had a thousand other titles. I remember one of them: Dame of the British Empire. They are sick for titles, the British. She was coming down this street, Hyde Park Gate, to see if there was anything she could do for "poor" Winston and his wife. They had first met years before at a dinner party in Lady Cynthia's family castle.

"I shall do whatever I am asked," Lady Cynthia said, speaking from her throat.

She said that in 1940, when Churchill said that people must fight the Nazis in the streets, she took out one of her father's old safari guns. "I'll have it spruced up," she told her husband. "Winston says we do have to kill them."

She had some woman, Mrs. Owens, walking with her who said, "Lady Cynthia has spent her life in public service."

"I'll have a cigarette before I go in," Lady Cynthia said.

"Only one is left," Mrs. Owens said.

"All to the good," Lady Cynthia said.

She took a filter-tip cigarette and stopped

to light it. Then she started striding again, the cigarette hanging from her mouth, the smoke streaming from her nostrils, her cane swinging as she came down the sidewalk to Winston Churchill's house.

There was a crowd and she said, oh, she would come another time, but a detective at Churchill's door took off his derby and offered his arm. I'm going to show you something. The detective's name was Murray. Sergeant Murray of Scotland Yard.

"You'll excuse me, I am sure," she said to me.

She went into the house and when she came out later I was right there waiting for her and she said, "Poor Winston, he's so old." She told me the wife was "bearing up well. Yes, wonderfully well."

She and Mrs. Owens went back up the street in the rain. I went right with them. I was not letting them out of my sight, particularly when I was the only person out of the huge crowd of news reporters who was following her. I wondered why her chauffeur hadn't brought the car right up to the house. Certainly, a Bentley. After all, she had the title to park on the sidewalk if she felt like it.

At the corner the two of them waited at a bus stop and Mrs. Owens went into her

purse for change. There is no big rich Bentley. Instead, a red double deck bus comes
up and they get on. I board, too, but with
a horrible feeling. Did she prefer riding
buses or, look out for this, could she be
broke? They took the bus to a neighborhood
of attached brick houses on miniature streets
in Chelsea. It is Queens, I told myself. Rego
Park. I searched the sky over the rooftops
for the spires of a great castle. Never. Lady
Cynthia's house is a small three-story brick
row house. The minute I set foot in the
house the cold air made me flinch. She
doesn't even have money for heat. The story
of my whole life. Nobody ever has any
money. Here is a woman they curtsy to and
she doesn't have forty dollars to her name.
A parlor maid, in blue dress and the cardigan sweater of a heatless house, took Lady
Cynthia's coat. A servant. I'm in *The Glass
Menagerie.* Lady Cynthia went into the living
room, a small room filled with papers and
books, and chairs and couches that looked
like the dust would explode if you sat on
them. The rug was good and worn. An
electric heater gave a faint glow in the tiny
fireplace. She had a brass bucket filled with
pieces of coal on the side.

Lady Cynthia pulled up her long skirt,
showing thick tan woolen knee-length socks.

19

Then she conducted her interview.

"You're a chief journalist, I expect?" she said, as if saying "*mahster* plumber."

Over the small mantel there was this enormous painting that covered the wall and was framed in gold and had a museum light. The plaque on the frame said, "P.P. Rubens." The title was *Le Jardin d'Amour.* How am I remembering this? Because there is no way you ever could forget it.

"It was hanging in the ballroom at our castle the night Winston came to dinner and met his wife," she said. "It's a magnificent work, isn't it?"

"Sure is."

"So many buxom women. I did considerable research on him. I wonder what the last wife looked like. She had to be a mere slip of a girl. She was just sixteen. You see, Rubens had decided that he had become old, and he should like to have someone scandalously young. I suspect she failed him. She was too thin for him to paint. She certainly didn't keep him alive."

"How much is it worth?" I asked her.

"Priceless," she said. With a good sniff.

I didn't think I was being boorish. After all, clearly she didn't have forty dollars to her name.

So I asked her, "How much would you take for it?"

When she didn't answer me, I said to her right away, because she was a classy old woman and I wanted to point something out, that she actually could afford heat in her house, and so I said to her:

"Somebody surely would pay you so much that, I don't want to get personal, but it would ease a lot of distress."

It was beneath her to answer. She was dead broke and living in the doorway of a gold mine but she was unable to pick up a shovel because she was shackled to the tradition of a family that had left her alone in hunger.

At this, Mrs. Owens cut in with great haste, "It's time for you to go, Lady Cynthia."

"Yes, I must go. I'm on a committee for an old people's home." She went up a flight of stairs, her legs pumping.

"Do you have an agenda for me?" she called over her shoulder to Mrs. Owens.

"She is very busy on committees," Mrs. Owens said. The doorbell rang and Mrs. Owens answered. A young woman in a proper suit stood at the door. Lady Cynthia came flying down. "Oh, yes. You're my driver."

The young woman driver said, "It must be awful, getting on these jaunts." And Lady Cynthia said, "Oh, yes, simply awful."

She turned around when she reached the sidewalk and she told me that I could stay and admire the portrait with the maid. Then she said, "But I do remind you that it is priceless."

Once, I asked the Metropolitan Museum of Art if they knew who now owned the Rubens. They suggested I try the Frick museum. I never checked on the painting after that, and I don't know how it got into my mind at this moment, although it is welcome. Lady Cynthia is long dead, but the painting is going to last forever.

Suddenly there was an explosion and two big gray doors with red and white emergency signs all over them flew open. The nurse walked first with her hand on the gurney and the attendant pushed and I went into a crowd of green.

2

When I first noticed my eye doctor walking along in the middle of the crowds that morning, he was about halfway up the street to my building. My street is Broadway, and next door, the butcher was out on the sidewalk in his roast beef whites with people brushing him. At the curb was a big red soft drink delivery truck for the supermarket. The driver struggled to push a hand truck through the streams of people. The number of people out on the street is startling even if you have been born here. Still, I was certain the eye doctor would spot me immediately and I retreated into the lobby of my building and sat in the dimness against the wall so that even if he walked up and pressed his face to the glass door he would be unable to find me.

I had my hand covering my left eye. The eyelid was down and I was seeing double. Which was the reason I was hiding from the eye doctor. I always hide from doctors, which is why this eye doctor, Robert Newhouse, was one of two who have looked at me. I had had eye trouble like this once before, only it was the right eye. At that time, the eye doctor said it was high blood sugar choking the sixth cranial nerve leading to the eye. The sugar attaches itself to the edges of the red blood cells, often making it difficult if not impossible for the red blood cells to flow into tiny areas where without the sugar they could travel with ease. The ridges of sugar on the red blood cells cause the cells to become piled up at a tiny passage such as the blood vessel feeding the sixth cranial nerve.

I did not like this discussion of sugar, which I felt would cause him, any word now, to blame me for my eye, so I immediately left and went to another doctor. He was Munro Levitzky and he was way over on the other side of the city, so I was sure that the two eye doctors never would see each other and fall into a deep discussion about me. The second eye doctor, Levitzky, had the nerve that time to refer to this condition as diabetes. I immediately left. I told him that I did not have diabetes and would enter no discussion of such a disease. Being sick with a disease involving sugar was something for people who eat candy bars or rice pudding or something like that.

Ice cream, not for a real guy. Although I am sixty-five, and I should not even have to type such a number because I have not missed a newspaper column since 1968 when I had a severe flu for two days, I still at this time wrote three columns a week, often four, for a New York paper that competed with three others, and did so in grand health because the excitement of my work snuffs out all germs. I have not had a common head cold in at least twenty-five years. Between columns, I have done a number of books and a play. Also, as I was telling the doctor, I had not been drunk in at least a few years, and have been generally away from alcohol for so long that I don't even think of it or notice a bar as I walk by. Therefore, as I assured the doctor, because alcohol was the only way I could contract diabetes, then I did not have diabetes.

At that time, as I was leaving the second eye doctor's office, he tried to tell me once more that I had diabetes. I pretended to listen intently, but could not wait to leave and forget it all, cockeyed right eye, lecture, doctor giving the lecture. Save your speeches for the weak.

I put on sunglasses that time and told everybody that my eye nerve was vibrating from chasing news on the streets. That sounded good. I'm in a nervous business, why shouldn't one of my eye nerves weaken? "I don't even have any medicine for it. He told me, just rest the eye," I said. The only reason I had no medicine was that there was none to take for it. Just wait. The eye might come back on its own, he said. Which it did. Eight weeks and the eye became normal.

And now, a few years later, here I am in my apartment building on Broadway with the other eye, the left, with a nerve condition. Of course I could not let the eye doctor passing by see me in such condition because I had completely disregarded his advice and warnings; I hadn't even seen him for at least two years. I waited in the dim lobby until he went by, after which I came out and started for the only kind of work I've ever done.

There is not a single solitary job in the world that is as good as the one I have at this moment. The money equals anything anybody in the history of the business ever earned. I invented the news column form and other papers immediately went out and hired imitators with Irish names. And at great prices. I was responsible for Irish names getting more money than any union since the founding of the wire lathers. To get here, I had to beat a rough, bleak, shrinking business. I started out in Queens County, where I was born, on the *Long Island Press*, which died after I left, as one of the last of the generation with no college and who came off the copyboy's bench. People at desks in the city room called out, "Boy! Copyboy." Or, "Oh, boy. Boy!" You were off the bench and running through desks to the guy calling you. He handed you folded copy written by typewriter to take to the city desk. Do not look at the copy while you move. Just get it there. I always imagined I was carrying a big bulletin story about a Staten Island ferryboat that just went down with 1,314 aboard in the middle of New York Harbor. Here I came between desks, my eyes wild with excitement; the copy I ran was four paragraphs about the Eastern Queens Civic Association.

Mostly when they called "Boy" they wanted a sandwich, a pencil, a container of coffee or clips from the library, which we called the morgue. After each run, you went back and sat on the bench and smoked cigarettes. Age? I was sixteen.

Now, on Broadway, going to work on this morning, a hand clamped over my left eye so I do not stumble into a bus, I decided I was not going to spend the day in the silver and gold of Manhattan. I thought that my face looked ruined and that people would stare me to death. I had to go into a black neighborhood, where the maimed and lame are so common that I'd be just another castaway. There also happens to be so much happening in one of these neighborhoods, so many shots fired, so many babies born, so many people fighting life while they go to work or beg for work, and all of this done while the people explain themselves with verbs that send sentences sliding along like loose change spilled on a polished floor. The only words that ever seem to stick in the ear come from neighborhoods like the one I decided to go to, South Jamaica, out in Queens.

I walked down Broadway to the subway at Lincoln Center. In the morning the Center is empty, with hoses washing the cement and pigeons strutting on the great plaza. The sun detonated on the great windows of the opera house and the sight of people inside was thrilling even when they were cleaning men. I bumped into a woman at the top of the subway steps, without noticing her. I took a bad step and swayed a little going down the staircase. An express train roared and rocketed through the station and the speed and noise convinced me to forget about it; you need two eyes to be around subways. I'll try tomorrow when I can see. I went upstairs and thought about what I was going to do, and at 68th Street I saw a cab and decided to use it.

We had a car in a parking garage on West 68th Street but that did me no good because I am the only man in New York City and maybe North America who does not drive. I never drove once in my whole life, either. Whenever people hear this, they ask right away, "You don't drive?" No. "Why not? Is it palsy?" No, I just don't drive. "Really?" Yes, I don't drive. "Have you ever driven?" Not ever. "Unbelievable."

My wife, who drives, once left me sitting in a car that was double-parked on Broadway, New York. It was parked nice. It had a delivery man snorting in a truck that was pinned against the curb.

"Yo."

"She'll be right out," I said.

"Only move up a few feet for me," he said.

"She took the keys inside with her," I said.

He stared down at the key ring hanging from the ignition.

"They're right in front of you."

I shook my head. "The truth is, I don't drive."

"The truth is, you move the effin' car or I get out of this effin' truck and I move you and the car."

"I'm telling you the absolute truth. I do not drive even a little bit."

"How come you don't drive and you still sit there and block the whole effin' street?"

"Because I like to sit and do nothing. I don't want to be bothered driving. I like to sit and do nothing."

My wife came out, waved in apology to the truck driver, and we went away.

I never had any need to drive. I was born in a gray frame house on 134th Street and 101st Avenue in Queens, a sooty neighborhood that had a bus right in front of the house, another bus two blocks down, an El, two subways, one of them the last stop of the famous A train, and maybe six blocks away, the Long Island Railroad, which rushed from Jamaica to Penn Station in Manhattan in fourteen minutes and cost nothing if you kept going through the cars ahead of the conductor; the trip was so short, he had to stop looking for tickets and tend to the doors pretty quick. Maybe once or twice when I first started working for a newspaper, I thought about saving for a car, but I needed all my money for beer. Just the smell of a good cold beer was a million times better than the overpoweringly musty odor of a used car. Besides, I would have been even money to hit something on any night and be in a funeral chapel thereafter. In all the years since then, I go after my news on the 2 train.

But on this day, my left eye shut, I take a cab to Jamaica to get my column. The driver began by going on 68th Street, which was lined with cars and double-parked vans in front of the four-story attached limestones and brownstones with high stoops. On the right was the elegant, gloomy old fieldstone Stephen Wise Synagogue. Next door, in a house with a high gray stoop, was Kathleen Turner.

The cab turned onto Central Park West. The driver drove down this splendid boulevard of old, ornate buildings lining one side of the avenue, with the trees of Central Park on the other. At 65th Street, he turned into the park and drove through a forest that was still green and the cab came rising up and out of the park and onto Fifth Avenue and went past the splendor of buildings that were put up for eyes to see, rich stone buildings of civilized height, twelve stories, with canopies in front and the sounds of birds in Central Park coming through the doors and putting music into the rich gold lobbies. Then past hotels where white-gloved doormen helped the rich take their luggage out of the car. We went over the Queensboro Bridge and along streets of the old stained factory buildings of Long Island City and onto a dreary expressway. The cab shot off it and onto Woodhaven Boulevard, past the tan fortress of Resurrection Ascension Roman Catholic Church, with lawns, church, grammar school, rectory and convent taking up the corner, and running up the street. We drove past blocks of two-story brick attached houses, the feet and legs of the middle class of the city. The houses ended at the thousands and thousands of graves at the St. John's cemetery. We were onto Atlantic Avenue, heading for Jamaica, and along streets of low factories and small shops and block after block of wood frame houses. We were on Liberty Avenue and 134th Street, which has two-story sand-colored corner buildings with stores on the ground floor, the stores with hand-lettered signs propped up in the windows. Down the narrow street that was lonely in the daylight was the gray frame house where I lived with my mother and father, who left the arena early, and my sister, grandmother, two uncles, and two aunts.

My mother never got over my father running out on her, although she had it in her to run somebody off like they were a strange dog. When it came to my father, I agreed with anything she said, and to her he was the same as dead. I told everybody in school that my father was dead. I was one of two in the class with no father. The other, Ernest Allingham, had a headstone to prove it. But then when my mother had a couple of drinks, suddenly she would say, "Do you ever see him?" I knew who she meant and I said no. "If I ever find you . . ." Then once, from out of nowhere, I answered the phone and he asked for my mother. He never said a word to me. He could have been too embarrassed, but that was his problem. I was bothered when he wouldn't talk to me on the phone. He hung on as if he were the cleaner calling about the wrong clothes being picked up.

I slept in a room with my uncle Jim, who was a bachelor and must have loved having me with him. Particularly when he tried to read while I was trying to sleep. I thrashed around to let him know and had him muttering real good. I never mentioned my father in just about my whole life. One night when the old Carson show was in New York and I used to walk over there in the late afternoon and go on it, for a taping to run late at night, there was a phone call from the NBC operator at about 1:00 A.M. They found me in Pep McGuire's saloon on Queens Boulevard. The operator said that a nurse had called from Miami to say that my father was in the hospital with a heart attack. Obviously they had just seen me on the show, which ran from 11:30 P.M. until 1:00. He's supposed to be sick, he's up in the middle of the night watching television. That freaking nurse. I had not even heard my father's name mentioned since I was six years old.

"Dear old Dad!" Fat Thomas yelled at the bar.

I went home and told my wife, Rosemary, who said after only a little hesitation, because we had a lot of kids and that costs, "You never picked him, but I guess we're going to have to pay for him." I called Jack Goldstein, who had left the police in New York and opened a private investigating business in Miami. Jack Goldstein went to the hospital and spoke to this man Breslin and he reported to me, sorry, it's really your father.

"Dear old Dad!"

I had Goldstein move him into St. Francis, a heart hospital in Miami Beach. Instantaneously, here was a letter from the hospital. Would I give two pints of my blood for my father? I was terrified of the idea of stretching out on a table and giving blood, especially for this effin' guy; a great big needle with a hose on it going in my arm. I would give him a bottle of red beet juice and tell him, here, Dad, try this. It's better than anything you have.

And I was going to do exactly that, except my friend Fat Thomas, as conciliator, said, "Buy him the blood." I called Jack Goldstein and asked him to price blood. "They give the derelicts fifteen dollars a pint," he said. I said, "I don't want a derelict. I just wanted to know how much it costs." He got me a price, I don't know what it was, thirty dollars a pint maybe. I asked him to buy the blood somehow, pay a donor, whatever. This was before the word AIDS, when donating blood was almost a casual act. I remember that I wired Jack Goldstein one hundred dollars on Western Union, and he got the blood. He would not be found handling things this small now. He has soared from private detective to owner of a sprawling Florida company, International Monitoring. Jack Goldstein checked the hospital daily and one morning he calls from Miami

Beach and says Breslin the elder is being discharged at three o'clock that afternoon.

Right away, I went to Western Union on Broadway and 40th in Manhattan and sent a straight telegram, on yellow paper, hand delivered right smack immediately:

BRESLIN, ST. FRANCIS HOSPITAL,

MIAMI BEACH.

NEXT TIME KILL YOURSELF.

YOUR SON.

A couple of times, he came back into my life like heavy snow through a broken window, and I will tell you about the other times later in this story.

My behavior is exactly what you get from somebody raised the way I was. I never remember my father for anything except how he would sit there and never say a word to me, and if we were out on a Sunday pretending to play football in Rufus King Park, he was in another world and all my excitement and enthusiasm trailed off into nothing. And I sat down on the grass and he just waited until it was time to go home. I remember him being bored more than I even do his fighting with my mother. When I grew up, my mother never kissed me once. Nor did I ever kiss her. When she was dying in the hospital I remember kissing her before I left at night. Otherwise, the closest we ever came to touching each other was when we sat together on the subway. I was a stranger who was out of her. My sister, Deirdre, at all times stronger, kept a daughter's tenacious love for the mother in thorny circumstances. She went on to a Ph.D. and a fine career in education and government. Of course I never remember my father kissing me. As everybody called my mother "Fran" and my father "Jimmy," I did the same. I never said "Mom" or "Pop." Everybody called my grandmother "Mother" and so did I. This made me the first kid in the neighborhood, maybe the only white kid at the time in all of New York, who spoke like the blacks, who also were being raised by the grandmother.

There was nothing complex underneath this. My family were people with winter emotions who could not use warm, affectionate words. How could they dare use any name that might show love?

The woman my father ran from, my mother, was a gifted woman who, when she was on the dry, could choose the precise behavior that would mortify others, and she did it with such pure joy that she could be thrilling to be around. My mother was a supervisor in the Department of Welfare's East Harlem office. One of the investigators was Martina Arroyo, who wanted to be an opera singer. My mother had her go into the ladies room and lock the door and vocalize for a half hour every afternoon. My mother wasn't alive to see Martina sing on the stage of the Metropolitan. Which was too bad, because in a dreary business, she always looked for a laugh.

One day, a few from her office came home in great glee, with my mother holding out this old fur coat on the end of a stick. She threw it onto the porch. Once, it had been a mink coat. Some weeks before this, a woman had flounced into the welfare office wearing the coat. "I be rich," she said. She was living in one room with her daughter and getting about thirty dollars a week from welfare. The woman told so many stories about the coat to so many in the streets that she soon made news: "Welfare Woman in Mink!" Politicians were beside themselves trying to express outrage in the newspapers. Only the *New York Post* said the welfare mink was a fraud. That was because the paper had about the only reporter who could cover welfare and tell the truth. His name was Joseph Kahn. Always, it seems, this city of so many and of such magnitude is told the truth by only one voice at a time.

So on this day on my old porch, while

my mother and the others were inside laughing, Al Hansen saw a great opportunity. He lived one house up. His father had a crane, which he parked in the yard with the boom high in the air. Each morning we all awoke with the shadow of manual labor across our faces. Al now presented the first Happening of his great life right here, at the front of my old house, where there was a dusty creaking porch running along the front and down one side, and with high hedges blocking the view of the sidewalk.

Al pretended to be a butler. He bowed and held the mink coat for me. I slipped into it. I had a loose T-shirt. He pulled the coat in front to make me snug. I stood up on the porch railing and held out my arms and flew off the railing in the mink coat. I was aiming at Al Hansen, who held the hedges open so I could fly through and onto the sidewalk.

In midleap I was hit by lightning in both armpits.

A white cloud of fleas from the welfare mink coat.

The welfare woman had found the mink in an empty lot in Harlem or whatever. I don't know how she wore it herself because there sure were a lot of fleas, green flies, hungry maggots in it.

I shucked the coat off and rolled in the dirt but that got rid of nothing. I had to go across the street to Tomasullo's gas station. I had so many fleas jumping out of my hair that he wouldn't come near me. He held out a tin can of kerosene and poured it over me.

Whenever there are stories and speeches about the outrages being committed by the poor against decent people, my armpits start to itch.

My mother's carefree attitude with something like a decayed mink was infectious. Then two drinks turned her eyes the color of iodine and she started in about my father, first keeping it inside her, with the air around her turning bitter, then with whispers to herself; one night, she stood in the living room and talked to herself aloud and almost hysterically. I sat on the staircase and peered through the banister. She was there for a long time, for hours, weeping and talking to her reflection in the big mirror. I dozed. It was getting late and I had to go to school in the morning. Suddenly a click woke me up. My mother was motionless. My eyes closed. There was another click and her weeping rose almost to a shriek and I saw that she had a pistol at her left temple.

I was up with a shout and starting down

the stairs. She spun around, hiding the pistol behind her back, and snarled at me: "You! Get back up there!"

She had said this "You!" to me so many times that I stopped, the way I was used to doing. I saw the pistol again and let out a great yell for my grandmother and continued down the stairs. I was grabbing and begging my mother for the gun and she was holding it away and she heard my grandmother coming down the stairs and her eyes left me and I just snatched the gun out of her hand. My grandmother took it from me, turned around and walked back upstairs.

My mother and grandmother did not get up until afternoon. Afterward, nobody ever mentioned in the house what had happened. The gun must have not been loaded. Or was it? I don't know. I think I was about eleven. The night was part of the dust in the air.

At school, the nun, Sister Anna Gertrude, was squalling about something; I had no homework with me and was missing books, something like that. I guess it was all for some test she was giving and I said I didn't feel well. She looked at me closely and then whispered, "Trouble at home?"

"Yes, Sister."

"Is it all right for you to go home now?"

"Yes, Sister."

"Then you can go."

That was it. "Yes, Sister." That was an excuse out of an abyss and it was received with sympathy and filled eyes no matter how frequently you used it. And I relied on it even in times where there had not been a murmur at home for weeks. As an excuse it was better than a car accident. Once you used this cry, it became an invaluable minor fraud that you always used. At the same time, at any moment when my mother snarled at me, I immediately reminded myself that I can use "Yes, Sister" with full conviction the next day.

Of course, this is the only way: turn anything bad into an advantage. Besides, young boys are as tough as dogs and they get over lacerations all right. If anybody wanted to admit this, soup kitchens would be packed with child psychologists. I also expanded the "Yes, Sister" to include writing something about the nastiness. All I ever wanted to do was write for a newspaper, and I realized early that bad news was great, even if it involved me. I protected myself by writing about it. Then I refined this as I grew older. It became my defense against anything that bothered me at all. I used work as an excuse to keep all storms in my life offshore — how can I discuss kids when I have to make a seven o'clock deadline?

This time, I went into the alcove in the living room where I used to hand-print a newspaper of little neighborhood notes I called "The Flash." It made me the Neighborhood Gossip. But this time I tried much more. As the story had more than one strand, it was complicated for me and took over a week. Now, when I finished "The Flash," I took it around to Worship's candy store and asked him to put it on the newsstand. My headline said, "Mother Tried Suicide." Later, I learned that the headline should have been in the present tense: "Mother Tries Suicide." Without looking, Worship said, "Put it out there yourself." He sold candy and booked horse bets. Worship was a small man who wore a gray truck driver's cap down over his forehead and had thick glasses perched on a sharp nose. He was behind the candy counter listening to the race results that came over all afternoon. After each result, he checked a betting sheet to see if any of his players had won anything. His wife, who had short hair and wore the uniform of the candy store owner, a drab dark red buttoned cardigan sweater, noticed my hand-printed "Flash" and said, "Let me see what you got." When I gave it to her, her face was alarmed. "Did this happen today?" she asked. I said no, that it had happened last week. "Then it's over," she said. Her face showed no expression as she crumpled up the paper. Usually when she did this with paper, it was bet slips, which she grabbed as police were either just outside or crashing in, and she popped the slips into her mouth, chewed them up while holding out a pack of Wrigley's to the cops. This time, the paper had something totally unimportant on it. A suicide that was a scratch.

She just threw the paper into the big oil drum they used for trash.

Here years later I look at another oil drum, and this time with one eye open. Flames lick the sides and men sit on broken-down chairs with their hands out for warming. They were on South Road in Jamaica, on the corner up from Adele's house, which was one flight over a closed bodega. Somewhere inside, at the top of the stairs, a child squalled and Adele shouted. Finally, she came down. She had large round pink curlers in her hair. A small boy, maybe four, wearing a heavy hooded blue jacket, clutched the skirt of her green coat. They walked three blocks to the corner food bank run by the Gordian Fellowship

44

Church. The food bank was in a mobile home set into an empty lot alongside the one-story stucco church itself. Adele came into the small and crowded food bank looking one way, pretending she didn't notice anything, while she shoved her boy forward. The man in front of them stuck out his hip to keep his place. He held an emergency food voucher from the welfare office up on Jamaica Avenue. I talked to him. His name was Harold Herndon and he had three kids of his own at home, in an apartment on Jamaica Avenue. He had been a caddie at the Seawane Club in Nassau County. He went back and forth by bus every day. The sun paled and the chill wind off the ocean closed the club for the winter. As caddying is off the books, he couldn't apply for unemployment benefits. There isn't a job for an unskilled black man from here to Bombay.

The woman working the counter was having an early lunch of her own, peanut butter and jelly on rye bread. Immediately, Adele's kid riveted his eyes on the sandwich. The woman food bank worker chewed nonchalantly. The kid's eyes went from the sandwich to the woman's mouth and back to the sandwich again. The woman picked up the sandwich for another bite. Never did her hand or mouth waver. She was a veteran food bank worker who knew that if she ever surrendered her personal food to a hungry look, she would be out there starving with the rest of them.

The worker went to the almost bare shelves in the room behind her. There were a few dented and outdated cans of meatballs and spaghetti, fruit cocktail, pineapple juice, chicken soup, salt, Carnation milk. She began an exercise in loaves and fishes. As she began to make up a bag for the old caddie, and the kid peering from behind him, more people walked into the food bank. Immediately, she had to cut down the amounts she was packing for the caddie and the kid.

I went back to the newspaper office on Park Avenue in Manhattan. I forgot about my eye being shut and I walked right into the glass entrance doors. I wrote the day's scene exactly as it was. I always figured that this was the only game; just go to any neighborhood where the poor live and tell the truth about what you see. Please do not put out a sermon; that is for Sunday. I finished at about 9:00 P.M. and I walked out of the building and onto Park Avenue, which had a lighted sky. I deserve something, a drink, a laugh over a drink, a big cigar over a beer, but I am afraid I'll lose the other eye so I

46

get nothing. I stepped out to get a cab and nearly was blown away by one cab speeding by. I reminded myself that I couldn't see and I better get home and sit in safety. Very carefully, I stood on the curb and waved for a cab. This can't continue, I decided.

I went to bed with the hope that a good night's sleep would cause the eye to open magically in the morning. But I was up at 4:30 A.M. and the eyelid was as tight as a security gate. There was a pain across the top of the left side of my head. I was making coffee with the television on, and this face on the screen called out, "Do you know what time it is? What are you doing up at this hour? You're drunk. Do you know where your wife and family are? You're strung out on alcohol or drugs. Why don't you try to save your family and yourself? If you want help . . ." He gave the phone number for a rehabilitation place he runs. I needed something a lot more sophisticated than a local call.

At eight o'clock, the eye still had pain around it and I went swimming in the pool on the second floor of my building. At this time, I swam a half mile early in the morning, and tried to do the same at seven at night. But I was disheartened. All that exercise and not a drop to drink and I am back with high blood sugar bothering my eye, just as it all started. This time, at 9:30, instead of ducking him, I was in the eye doctor's office on West 60th Street.

He was Robert Newhouse and he spent some time with a light peering into my left eye. "Freaking blood sugar," I muttered. He said that while blood sugar could be the cause, he also was thinking of an aneurysm. He thought I should get an MRI to see if this was the cause. An MRI stands for magnetic resonance imaging and we will get to that later. He took out a prescription pad and wrote "MRI — for possible aneurysm." It was just a conversation in an office. A major flood announces itself with little tree twigs in the first fingers of water that do not yet seem angry.

I did not know what an aneurysm was. I thought it was something like an embolism, although that was murky to me, too. I did remind myself that the only time I ever saw the words *aneurysm* and *embolism* was in obituaries. Dr. Newhouse told me that an aneurysm was a bulge in an artery up in the brain and that they fix it by clipping it.

The common quality of the word *clip* caused me to nod and get up to go. There must be nothing extraordinary about it.

I started by going home and calling my

friend Peter Johnson, the lawyer. He does a lot of medical suits and he knows a lot of the terms and doctors. I know many doctors, too, but I never show up for appointments and hide for years at a time and as a result I am afraid even to call somebody. In particular, I couldn't call Kevin Cahill, whom I haven't seen in ten years, or Norman Wikler, at New York University Medical Center, because I am a full year late with him.

"What did the eye doctor say you had?" Peter Johnson asked me.

"Oh, the guy said something about an aneurysm."

"Aneurysm. Are you nuts? Stay there. Don't you move."

When he called me back, he gave the name of Mark Kupersmith, a neurological ophthalmologist, at NYU Medical Center.

"He is a huge name," Johnson said.

"Who do I say sent me?"

"We got Norman Wikler to call him. He's a very big doctor at NYU."

My wife and I took a cab over to NYU Medical Center, which is on First Avenue, with the East River running behind it. The entrance to the building was crowded with cabs and cars and I got out of the cab directly in front of the blue brick medical examiner's building next door. On the steps there was a woman with a gray face and tears talking to two men in zipper jackets. She had a husband inside in the morgue, that was clear.

Kupersmith came into his office, young and hurried, as it was the end of the day and he had run up from the Eye and Ear Infirmary on 14th Street. He immediately examined me at length, as befits his most impressive title. It turns out that there are only three people in his specialty in the entire city, which means that there are probably none in the country, and it is merely the medicine of the future. He had me follow his finger, walk one foot in front of the other, follow a light. He said he did not believe it was an aneurysm because the pupil of the left eye was small and unaffected by any pressure from within. If the right pupil had been small and the left enlarged it would have been the signal for immense trouble. An aneurysm or tumor pressing on something and causing the pupil to swell. But the pupil was small. Therefore, every classic sign pointed to the third cranial nerve of the left eye being tormented and frozen by elevated blood sugar.

Kupersmith thought it would be wasteful for me to get a test as expensive as an MRI. He said he was not going to have me running up a bill just because I have half a name in the city.

"You'd know if you had an aneurysm causing your eye," he said. "You'd have the worst headache in your life. That is the symptom." He said that an aneurysm, this bulge in the wall of an artery, fills with more and more blood over the years. The blood coursing through arteries is rough on the artery walls. If one gives, and this aneurysm, this balloon, forms, the rushing blood over time causes the balloon to swell and the balloon skin to weaken more. With much blood collecting in the sac, each heartbeat causes the blood to swirl angrily against a thinner and thinner balloon and one day the aneurysm bursts.

What is most noticeable about a burst aneurysm is a new body in the morgue or an unconscious form in an emergency room. Before that worst headache, there is no sign at all of the trouble. Some even believe that it is possible for people to have an aneurysm at birth, and have it burst at an early age. That is why a high school baseball player drops dead while running from first to second base. Dr. Kupersmith was saying, "Half the people with aneurysms that burst never make it to the hospital. Of the fifty percent that do survive, only one half are aware of very much. The rest, that's twenty-five per-cent, are listed as fine." His face and tone indicated that those listed as fine had the spirit of wallpaper.

"You can die from an aneurysm," I said, sagely.

"If you're lucky," the doctor said. "You don't want to know what happens if you don't die from one of these things."

He gave me Tylenol with codeine and sent me home.

This was on a Tuesday evening, October 25, and he said he was leaving the city for a conference on Friday, the 28th of October.

I knew that date because my son Patrick was to marry Maria Smith on Saturday, October 29. On Friday night, the 28th, we were having a dinner party for forty people, the immediate families of both bride and groom.

After leaving Kupersmith's office, my wife and I were getting off the elevator at the first floor, when she looked at a woman pushing a man in a wheelchair onto the next elevator. "Isn't that Abe Rosenthal?" she said.

I kept walking.

"Yes, it is," she said. "I can tell by the back of his head."

At which point in the elevator, the woman

pushed the wheelchair around and Rosenthal, sitting in pajamas and a robe, looked right out at me.

We are almost mortal enemies. At one time he was the editor of the *Times* newspaper and I wrote columns for a paper called the *Herald-Tribune* about life in a large saloon on Queens Boulevard called Pep McGuire's. The hatcheck girl was Mickey Burke, whose husband, Jimmy Burke, stood near the door. Burke was a promising criminal, who soon was to be famous for holding up the Lufthansa Freight Terminal for close to nine million. He tarnished the endeavor by killing almost everyone who could link him to the crime. Which was a waste because they got him anyway. Another great rookie, John Gotti, was around to see Burke now and then.

Pep McGuire's was a place out of the 1920s and '30s with more murderers and judges per foot of the bar than any place the city had seen in years. But since it was in Queens, nobody knew anything about it. Every time I mentioned it, people thought it wasn't true. Mostly, this was because of insane jealousy. Rosenthal announced that I was making everything up. He showed up one night with Bob Price, then a deputy mayor of New York. When they walked in,

Fat Thomas was roaring at the bar. He was six-three and weighed 415 pounds. A deep voice carried the length of a block. His hair was slicked straight back and he wore thick glasses and had a chin that was part of his neck. The bartender had been too slow for him so he had gone behind the bar himself. Rosenthal thought Fat Thomas was the bartender and ordered a drink. Fat Thomas poured himself a half glass of scotch, swallowed it and walked off.

He had fifty-one arrests for bookmaking. He knew the whole world by initials. One night, I introduced Fat Thomas to Norman Mailer and Fats said with great familiarity: "How is IB for Brooklyn?" And Mailer said, "My father is fine." IB for Brooklyn was the senior Mailer's code when he called in bets.

One of Fat Thomas's arrests was for assault on four policemen. This occurred when they banged on the door of the apartment where Fat Thomas was manning the phones for horse bets.

"Yes?" Fat Thomas said.

"Bread man."

"Just leave it at the door," Fat Thomas said, gathering up bet slips. "Western Union" or "bread man" always meant cops. He stuffed his mouth with the slips and opened the window.

"Open the door or we'll break it down and then break your head," they called.

Fat Thomas went out the window. He got one foot on the fire escape. Which swayed. He sighed, pulled his leg back in and ran into a closet in the bedroom. The door now came flying open and the four cops rushed in, saw the open window onto the fire escape and raced for it. One, two, three, four, they bounced onto the fire escape. The thing gave way and the four went crashing to the alley. There were broken ankles, sprained ankles and charges that Fat Thomas had tried to murder police.

Now Fat Thomas was real, alive and barging around Pep McGuire's. Back in the office, Brother O'Connell, bank robber, sat at the desk and cleaned a machine gun.

Seeing this, Rosenthal said, "It's all true!" He wound up with so much whiskey in him that he threw himself at a huge blond Lufthansa stewardess. He buried his head into her chest.

"Abe, she wants to throw you in an oven," Fat Thomas said.

"I know. I can't help it," Rosenthal said.

And that is the truth. Now he writes a column for the *Times* newspaper. The last time I saw him we were on a shuttle plane from Washington and I walked past his seat and he looked right through me. All I had done to him was leave a message for him at the *Times* newspaper that his column was an embarrassment and how could he ever have stood at the bar with me and pretended to be an equal?

"Rosenthal!"

"Breslin!"

I saw that the woman pushing the wheelchair was his wife. He motioned to her to hold the elevator door open. I rushed up to him and the two of us hugged and kissed each other out of the immense relief of being alive.

I remembered that late one afternoon I was at the bar of Gallagher's Restaurant on West 52nd Street with Rosenthal and Dick Dougherty, the deputy police commissioner, and we were talking about newspapers and I had this big cold beer in my hand in the lights and bright polished wood and I just said out of nowhere, "I don't have to keep chasing fires for a living. I'm going to do a book called *The Gang That Couldn't Shoot Straight*." The title is one of the three or four most repeated titles of my time. And I always wondered what caused that to come out of me so perfectly. It wasn't just the beer, although drinking can carry an idea better than most other things. This time, the words flew out like a prayer learned while young and thus forever. Of course it happened like this because of the energy coming from smart people at a good bar, and Rosenthal sure was one who was there.

Now, he had just had several heart bypasses. He said he had gone to his doctor and complained that his legs seemed too heavy to move and the doctor said it wasn't the legs, that he needed a bypass and right away. "Forget the world, the column, everything," Rosenthal said. "I'm taking care of myself until I'm better." His wife nodded.

"What's the matter with you?" he asked.

"Nothing," I said. I am well and he is sick.

The guy once caused newsrooms to quiver and presidents to wonder how they could fend off his anger and appeal to his vanity and humor. Now he was waving good-bye from a wheelchair. If he couldn't do the wave, people would be waving good-bye to him. I had a warm feeling about him. If illness was the reason for this, then it was wrong; I should have liked the guy all along on his brains alone.

As I was leaving NYU on this Tuesday night, I stopped and swallowed the first two of my codeine pills at the water fountain in the lobby. By the time I got home at Broad-

way and 68th Street, I was walking back-
wards. I do not have the physical ability to
be much of a drug user. The codeine pills
had me in a stupor all week. On Thursday
night, October 27, I was awake most of the
night with a sharp pain all over the left side
of my head. I did not have to leave the
house for a column on Friday so I stayed
home and took codeine. But when my head
was still throbbing on Friday afternoon, I
called Kupersmith at NYU.

He said, "Gee, I don't like to hear about
a pain this long after seeing you. I'll tell you
what, if you still have the pain on Monday,
maybe you ought to come in for an MRI."

"I'll be right down there," I said.

The doctor said, "It's already five-thirty
on a Friday."

"I'll come right down anyway."

"Wait a minute. We have to get an appointment for you."

"Good. I'll be there by six o'clock."

At this moment, my house was crowded
with people setting up for the wedding dinner party. When I announced that I was
dashing to the hospital, there was an immediate, extraordinarily sullen reaction. I am
usually uncomfortable, sometimes frantically so, with any family celebration. What
I usually do is remind myself of some

wretched experience as a child, dwell on it until I become so sick from head to toe that I retreat from the warmth and humor of the day and take to my bed until the celebration is gone and forgotten. My holiday tradition is to climb into bed on Christmas Eve and not get out until New Year's. So at this moment, everybody in the family thought that my sudden need to get an MRI at a hospital was just some more cheap malingering.

And now, for this Friday wedding dinner, my wife looked up from the bright white napkins and silverware shining in the lights and she said to me, "This is your son's wedding. Don't you care about it?"

I said, "I do. I also care about my head."

With that, I left. I promised to be back for most of the dinner, but nobody believed me.

The cab I was in did not go five blocks and I was looking out at Central Park when I suddenly found the headache was gone. Right away, I stir in the back. If there is no headache, then it was all in my mind to begin with and the mere act of heading for a hospital caused the pain to evaporate. The cab was about to turn into Central Park at 65th Street. There was a red light there, just before the turn, and I figured that if the cab had to stop for the red light, I would pay him and jump out and go home. I was digging into my pants pocket for the cash to pay him when the light turned green and the cab swung into the park. I sat back and the cab went to the East Side and the hospital. The NYU radiology department was in the basement of the hospital entrance that has a door to the parking garage on 30th Street and First Avenue. Next door, on the steps of the medical examiner's office, two men gestured with their hands in a sign of helplessness. They had trouble, and I had nothing wrong with me; maybe a fraudulent headache brought on by a memory lurking in the bottom of my stomach.

In the basement waiting room of the radiology department, there was a woman behind a counter who was attending to a small man in a gray zippered jacket. He smiled in befuddlement as he and the woman went through these papers, the records of his life, that he had placed on the desk. I sat on one of the plastic seats. Next to me, a heavy woman chewed on a sandwich and the child seated next to her drank orange soda from a can. I'll be here forever, I told myself. I'll blow the whole dinner at home. I was talking to myself about getting out of the place when I heard the woman behind the desk say, "No, through that door." The old man in the jacket was spinning around in the middle of the room and smiled as he saw the right door. The woman looked at me and nodded. I was surprised that I was next. I had no hospitalization cards with me. I gave the woman my credit card. The cost of the MRI was $1,320.

A short, pleasant man in a white jacket looked into the waiting room, called my name, and had me follow him into this large cool room that at first seemed like a television control room. Silent forms in white coats hunched over computer terminals and tapped the keys. And all along the walls, colored lights on the monitor screens blinked. Now and then one of them would emit a musical tone. The short man helped me into an alcove and onto a table. With a hum, the table slid me into a tight white tunnel whose outer surface was an electromagnet that seemed big enough to pull a bus. A voice on a loudspeaker told me not to move. He could have saved his breath; there wasn't room for me to scratch my nose.

This white tunnel was the third and sharpest way that we have to see through the cloud banks inside the body without tearing it open like a package. The first is the X ray, which picks out cracks in bones, and pneumonia. The tremendous advance from this was the CAT scan, which can move from bone to soft tissue. This third looking glass, the MRI, doubles the sight. The MRI gives such definition that its camera can pick out the softest of tissues, the nerves, the brain. The MRI uses magnetic force, and radio waves on the hydrogen atoms of the fat and water of the body. The variations in amounts of water show in the tone and texture of what can be seen on MRI film. The nucleus of each hydrogen atom spins at angles it chooses. When the great magnet is turned on, it causes many of the nuclei to act as if they were drafted. They suddenly line up and spin at the same angle. The MRI machine sends radio signals that cause the hydrogen atoms to fall out of line as they absorb the waves. When the radio signals are turned off, the nuclei, feeling this hand lifting from the shoulder, go back into line, this time spraying the energy from the radio waves. On this great MRI machine surrounding nuclei, atoms, body, a receiver catches the energy. After which it all becomes the unexplainable. The receiver sends the energy patterns onto a computer to be analyzed. While these silent forms in white coats sit at the computer terminals near the

MRI and tap keys, somewhere in another room, inside a great big bin, the main computer holds the radio energy patterns right up to its nose, sniffs, takes a bite and chews thoughtfully with its little electronic teeth, and thinks the whole thing onto a cable to the computer terminal inquiring the most persistently in the MRI room. Where suddenly on the computer terminal screen the inside of the body turns into bright large images that doctors gaze at intently, looking for the deadly while the patient sits up from the machine and puts on his clothes, hoping to leave.

I am on my back in the MRI machine and I begin to see images of the little guy who started all this. His name was I. I. Rabi and he won a Nobel Prize for his work on magnetic imaging. The man must have saved ten million from operations, and uncounted lives. Although he did not happen to save so many other lives on two of his other big physics projects. He was a consulting engineer on the first atom bomb detonated at Los Alamos, New Mexico. He won the scientists' gambling pool for the size of the explosion of that first one. He bet the explosion would be almost equal to 18,000 tons of dynamite and when the bomb went off and the sky turned weird, he was closest and won $116. He also worked in a laboratory at MIT in Cambridge, Massachusetts, on the underwater radar that helped cover the face of the Atlantic with dead German sailors from submarines. Here you had continents deep in war, with men turning into killers everywhere, and one of the most dangerous of all was a little man nobody noticed who commuted by train from Cambridge to Los Alamos, and stayed two months or more, and never told his wife where he was.

When I met him, he lived up on Riverside Drive in a big Columbia University faculty apartment and I think he was one of the three or four close friends I was able to make over my first thirty years of writing newspaper columns. Rabi could talk straight through dinner and refuse to bore. The first time I met him was at his apartment over a column I was trying to do and that led to a date for dinner at the Café des Artistes on West 67th Street, one of the two or three most sumptuous places in New York. I said something about Reagan being insane for pushing for Star Wars, and Rabi shook a finger at me.

"I tell everybody, 'Don't deny an old man his dreams.' The more you oppose him the more stubborn he'll get. If you let him indulge his dreams, the whole thing will go away of its own."

"Because it won't work?"

"Sure it works. Do you want me to tell you how? Here is Star Wars. You have a pitcher on the mound. You have to shoot the ball out of his hand at the instant of release. If you shoot the ball before he releases it, it is no good. If you shoot it after he releases it, it is too late. You must shoot the ball at the moment of release. Oh, it can be done. Except that you stand there waiting for twenty years and go crazy.

"Everybody knows this. I talk to the Russian scientists. We all talk to each other. There are no real secrets. But money is more important than sense. The generals and the defense contractors use Russia as an excuse for making huge profits. The scientists in Russia tell the government there that the whole idea is crazy. But the generals go to the Kremlin and they tell them, 'The scientists are wrong. Look at all the money the Americans are spending on this system. If they spend their money, there has to be something to it. We must start building one immediately.' "

He wrecked one celebration we were having at Costello's by calling my office and saying that he wanted to come immediately to the "Pub" and his wife called saying that she was nervous about him tripping or falling because he was old and as thin as a straw. When he came in, he got right up on a barstool and of course it was rickety and even a feather-light guy like this could make it rock and tip. I missed so many drinks because I was holding on to the stool that I went home sober.

The last time I saw him, just before he died a couple of years ago, he was at a table at the old Brownsville Children's Library on Dumont Avenue in Brooklyn. He had been born and raised on Hopkinson Avenue in Brownsville, which for so long gave such energy and talent to the city and country. But that was a white city then, and now it is all changed; changed utterly. The schools are frozen by color fear; when you put a white teacher in front of a black class the teacher generally can't teach and the pupils figure that the teacher doesn't like them anyway so why pay attention?

On the way to the library, we passed the Danny Kaye Junior High School on Sutter Avenue, and the sound of a rap shouter on the radio was going all over the street. The words were impossible to hear, as any white could tell you.

Danny Kaye, raised on these streets, came

exploding, crashing, skyrocketing onto Broadway with his brilliant: "Gadeeep gat gizzle, gadeep gat go. . . ."

Rabi, cringing, thought the rap was atrocious and Danny Kaye a legitimate legend around the world. The car stopped for a moment in front of the school. There was a cluster of students with heads rocking to the rap song. I pointed to the name over the school. "Who was Danny Kaye?" I ask a young girl. A shrug. "Wasn't he a white guy?" another girl asked. Yes, he was, I said. "Then he doan mean nothin' to me."

Rabi and I then went to the Brownsville Children's Library. We were there because one day I asked him if he ever had been back to his old neighborhood and he said, "You'd need a tank to go there." I told him that was ridiculous and he had no right to speak like that as long as he had reached this level in his country. I told him, "Every time I go to any of these places, a crowd comes around me the minute they see my notebook because they think that I am connected to an official office somehow and that I have jobs. That's all they care. 'You taking down names for jobs? Put my name down for a job.' " He decided to go with me. The Brownsville library was the place where, at age nine, he had learned to use science books. Once, he ran to a hardware store on Pitkin Avenue and the man gave him old bits of wire and a tube or so and he made a radio.

Looking back on it, I don't know how I could justify to myself bringing him there. Like I was so tough that I could defend him from the street right outside the window, which had on the south side the Tilden Houses and on the north the Brownsville Houses, both places at this time being frantic from gunfire.

But his childhood library drew out of Rabi the simplicity of thought that is at the heart of every genius. He looked around at the books on this day and said, "It is a fact that we have free speech in this country. But everyone is afraid to use it."

Afterward we went to Peter Luger's, a restaurant that sits amidst the old Williamsburg tenements right at the foot of the bridge that goes over the river to the Lower East Side of Manhattan. Luger's is probably the best steak house in New York. When Rabi and I went to lunch in Luger's, the little man was so busy eating that he said nothing. Rabi ate so much and against every dictum of his doctor that he could barely move.

And now, in this MRI room, I wished

that Rabi were here to make sure his invention that saved so many would announce that there was nothing wrong with me. At this point, the white tunnel emitted a series of sounds that were the equal of an El train passing right over my head. As happens each time anything threatens me, I closed my eyes and fell asleep. This is an uncomplicated act. At this time, I could not believe that there was the least bit wrong with me beyond the nerve going to the left eye. But also, somehow, this great machine with its sinister noise just might discover something horrendous. Oh, of course this is impossible. But just to clear the whole thing out of my head, let me close my eyes and drop into sleep. Which I did.

I woke up to footsteps on the clean tile floor. The table I was on slid me out of the tunnel and the radiologist said I could get up. I was putting on my shirt when he came back and told me that there was neither tumor nor aneurysm bothering the nerve to my left eye. I had absolutely no reaction to this, other than to start buttoning my shirt. Of course there was nothing wrong. What was I supposed to expect? The guy saying, "Too bad. You lose. You die"?

I rushed home to the dinner party. When everybody asked me how I was, I gave a dismissive wave and said I was in most magnificent health and that we all should talk about tomorrow's wedding. Through the rest of the night and through the next day's dazzling wedding, I was a tremendously pleasing social companion. I talked to the men about gangsters and sports. I was so gracious to women and children that I even baffled myself.

I started the week after the wedding by writing about the election. Years of gunfire on streets like Dumont Avenue in Brownsville, and reports of it circulating around the nation, caused many in New York to sigh, just as they did in congressional precincts in Georgia and Florida, and say, without using the actual words, "Please make the blacks go away."

At the start of the week, the doctor from NYU, Kupersmith, was away at the conference he had told me about. Which didn't matter, because the entire business of my health was over as far as I was concerned. The MRI had told me so.

At noon on Thursday, November 3, Kupersmith's secretary called me at my house. She asked me to hold on. There was flashing and nothing happened. Her voice came in quickly. "Hold on." More flashing. This is exactly how they tell you in stories about hearing the bad news from a doctor, I told myself. I wondered what people involved felt like. Of course this has nothing to do with me. After much flashing, Kupersmith came on the phone. I was ready to say that I was fine, which of course I knew was what he was calling about, but he started talking first.

"We were right in saying that there was no aneurysm or tumor affecting your left eye. But then the doctors took time to study the whole MRI film, not just the portion on your left eye. And in a completely unrelated place they have noticed what seems to be a bulge. We had a conference about it. It could be a strange formation of the brain that was there when you were born. Others are afraid of an aneurysm. Nobody is sure. We want to take more tests. What appears to be the bulge is directly in the front and we should be able to find out what it is."

"It is directly in front of what?" I asked.

"The front of the brain," the doctor said. "But they have a way of treating that."

"What do they do?" I asked.

"A brain operation," the doctor said.

Right away, I went for the first thing that came into my mind to try and pull myself out.

"Nothing hurts me," I said. "I haven't

had any pain in what, a week?"

"I told you that you don't feel anything," he said. "Then you get the worst headache of your life."

I said, "You know, I was in this riot in Brooklyn and I got hit and I had to go to an ophthalmologist."

That night in Brooklyn happened to have changed the way people live and think in New York more than any other in my time. All I wanted to do at first was write about the night as accurately as possible so everybody at least would know one more thing. This night was a full year ago before now. But I clutch any part of the past that might show that anything amiss with me is easily explainable, thus reducing the matter to the importance of dust in the eye. Make something other than what it is. Perhaps my explanation would have Kupersmith suddenly asking me, "Where were you hit? Right between the eyes you say? Show me? When was this?"

But live on the phone now, he ignored this and went on to talk about something called an angiogram. Yet, I could not wait to tell him about the night in Brooklyn because it was such a prominent one that perhaps its effects still were to be assessed.

"White man in a cab," they had suddenly

called out that night from a street corner on Utica Avenue in Brooklyn.

Up ahead, two blocks up, was Eastern Parkway, the big main street where I was heading to watch the mayor at a meeting over street disturbances that were going on. The night before, a car driven by a young member of the Lubavitcher Orthodox Jews had run over a seven-year-old boy, Gavin Cato, who was black. The rumors ran shrieking through the black streets. A crowd of young people who were black surrounded a young Jewish student and stabbed him. At the hospital, the mayor and the other politicians jammed into the trauma room and soothed the student, Yankel Rosenbaum, and the medical residents were too intimidated to shout them out of the small space. They couldn't fit a portable X-ray machine into the space and therefore nobody saw the wound in Rosenbaum's back. By the time they noticed it upstairs, it was too late. He died of others not knowing enough to stay out of the way of critical work.

Two nights later, the cab I'm riding in suddenly is running into a wall of young black kids. I tell the cabdriver to back up and get out of here. The cabdriver, who was black and I mention this because color sure counted for nothing for him, rolled the cab back at about two miles an hour. That was the end of that. Into the cab they piled, the young and the angry. "Money, money, money. Gimme, gimme, gimme." I saw the cabdriver being pulled out of the front seat and into a thunderstorm of fists. Hands from both sides ripped at my pants pockets. One of these young guys was up on the hood of the cab and he swung a baseball bat at the windshield. There was no loss of reason or momentary blindness to the world. This was a permanent fury, flames from so long ago licking everything inside him. He swung the bat until the windshield turned seafoam green. Now on the hood he looked through the open windshield at me. He wanted to step through that window and get a swing at me, I could see that.

There was no way for him to get me. There were so many of them piled into the backseat with me that he had no real target. They were throwing punches, holding me, ripping at my clothes for the only thing they wanted at the moment, money.

My head was down and there was this small narrow view of open space between the car door and somebody's hip, and I reached up and grabbed the hair of whoever it was and with scared strength I pulled him right down and went for that door head first and wound up popping through others and onto the sidewalk, where I started to straighten up and I was hit with a thousand punches. Whether I wanted to or not, I stayed right in the middle of the crowd and that was fortunate. Police tell me later that at least two of them had guns, but they could not shoot me because a gunshot would have hit one of their own in the crowd just as easily as it hit me. Could have gone right through me and into somebody else, too.

I had one grim thought. "Once too often."

Yes, I had gone once too often to the well and found it was filled with gasoline and the flame shot up and scorched my face. That is a good way to express it because right now the street was orange and hot from the cab that was burning in the street alongside me.

Now I shrieked to myself, Look for the knife. I know I took one real good smack when I was trying to see a knife in the many hands. The only sounds were feet shuffling, grunting, yipping, and these voices:

"White bastard."

"White mothereffer."

"Look out, look out. Let me kill him."

"Smoke him. Smoke the effin' dude."

I guess I am about halfway down queer street because of all the punches, but at the same time there is nothing unusual about hearing what they are saying. Of course they want to kill me. They kill each other all week long. If I was hearing these words and the emotion of them for the first time, I would have died on my own right there or been so immobile that I would have been beaten to death. But out of plain familiarity, up I came from that sidewalk.

Right in front of me now was this shop and a man and woman standing in the doorway and just as I raised myself to dash in, the big corrugated electric gate came down. The last thing I saw was the legs and feet of the owner and his wife as they stood in the doorway and the big thick gate slammed to the street and left them safe inside and me out on a sidewalk with a mob all around me.

An older voice called out, "Leave him alone."

"That's all. Get away from him," another older voice said.

Then these two guys stepped up to me. One of them was showing a knife as big as a pitchfork. The guy with the knife took me by the arm and led me out of the crowd. The rest of me was reeling, a flag blowing in a stiff wind. The other older guy, chubby and in a blue shirt, said, "Remember me? You were in the bookstore."

I don't know how I knew, but I said, "Fifth Avenue."

"That's right. I'm the security. You was talking to me."

Now I was led stumbling down the sidewalk and away from the crowd and we went silently down the street, past these older people who just stared at me. They had not dared to come any further along the block.

Now I saw that two blocks away was the precinct, the 77th. A couple of cops walked out as far as the parking lot entrance. They had blue crash helmets and raincoats held under one arm. They looked at me walking unevenly, the guy still holding on to me. He told me that his name was George Valentine. He kept saying, "You're all right now. You're all right now."

And one of the cops, in his forties, an Irish name in the suburbs I would bet my house, called out, "What do you think of your friends now?"

The other cop said, "You wanted them. Now you got them."

I muttered something but they walked back into the lot and to the back door of

the precinct so I couldn't look at their name-
plates.

We stood on the curb and a gypsy cab
with a pounding muffler pulled up. We got
in and went to Manhattan. We were crossing the bridge when I remembered Rabi. I
had told him the truth, that these streets
always had been about as ominous as a
summer beach. This time, he could have
been in fragments; that notebook I had with
me tonight didn't impress the people out
there.

At this time, I lived on the corner of
Central Park West and 67th Street. The
building was somber and staffed. Three
doormen inside the glass doors told you all
you had to know about the price of the
place. Central Park was the other side of
the street. There were benches on the sidewalk along a low fieldstone wall, and hanging over the wall were branches of the
London plane trees and lovely maple trees
that run along the wall for a couple of miles
and fill the park inside. The trees were still
deep green on this fall night. A roadway
goes through the park, passing little white
lights sprayed all over the tree branches like
new buds, and covering every brick of the
old, sumptuous restaurant, the Tavern on
the Green, that sits at the end of the drive.

It had to be dazzling for Valentine and the cabdriver. Upstairs, my wife gasped when I walked in with Valentine behind me. Both eyes were mostly closed. I got some money out for the cab fare and for Valentine and he gave me a phone number, which of course would be no good.

My wife put in an emergency phone call to the ophthalmologist, Munro Levitzky, who thus received his first summons to riot duty in his thirty years of practice. While we waited for him to call back, I flopped into a tub and held my face in the warm water. Strong thing, a face, I thought. Just by soaking the bruises, I felt they were immediately improved. When I got out, I said that all I really needed was an old-fashioned towel filled with ice that a bartender hands to the loser in the fistfight. But my wife said the left eye looked like it was getting worse and when the ophthalmologist called back she made an appointment to meet him right away at the NYU emergency room over on First Avenue. There, in a dark room, the doctor looked at my blood-covered eyes for some time and allowed as how a punch to the cheek forces the blood up into the eye, which was why mine was coated with blood.

And so now, a whole year later, I am on my way to the hospital to see Dr. Kupersmith, and I thought of the night in Crown Heights as a simple explanation for the blotch on my MRI. Great! Then it suddenly gave me an empty feeling to rely on this as an explanation. Let me try anyway. The first thing I did was to start talking to Kupersmith about the eye being smacked shut during a huge riot.

He shakes his head.

"Nothing to do with it," he said.

He made an appointment for an angiogram on the following Monday.

The test would take nine or ten hours of Monday, and that was a column day. The column runs on Tuesday but you always call the day before "the column day." This time, I spent much of Sunday writing something on the political campaigns formalizing the middle class, making the status absolutely official, as if we finally had become British. I didn't finish but I had enough written now to finish it up before the deadline on Monday, probably after the angiogram. Besides, I despise anything for a newspaper that is written in advance of the day it is used. Words for a newspaper come from nervous energy on a deadline, and a reader can feel it resonating from the story he is reading. Why rob him and put out something that is stale? My notion was to have something right out of that day in the column.

Now, at 5:00 P.M. on this Sunday, I put on a suit and tie and went down to St. Francis of Assisi Church on 31st Street, right off Seventh Avenue. It is a gloomy redstone building that is the criminal court of the Catholic Church. This is the arena where the old offenders, the recidivists, the outright guilty, go in those moments when a fire suddenly resumes at the bottom of the ashes of guilt and sends the sinner running like a firefighter back to his beginnings: up the church steps and on his knees inside the first open confessional booth.

They hold confessions at St. Francis all day and night. The priest's name is on a plate, lit by white light, over the middle door of the confessional. A small red light indicates that a penitent is being heard in one of the two confessional booths. If there is no priest in any of the booths, all you have to do is press a bell and soon one will come through a door in the back of the church and walk to a confessional and open up for trade.

It had been several years since I had confessed in church. In that time, I had established my own rules for being a Catholic. I would fail to attend mass for weeks. When

I'd finally show up, I would say an Act of Contrition and at communion time stand up and go on the line to the altar. It happens that this is against all rules. A sinner must formally confess before receiving communion. Only if you are in the state of Grace, which means that there are no sins of any sort on your soul, a rule that means the lines for communion would be sparse at best and empty at normal, can you receive communion without a tongue light with truth, and the soul beneath bright with inner light from confession.

Usually, however, I had no choice but to say a prayer and get up. These communions by my own rules were usually at family weddings or funerals or celebrations and I could not just sit there while everybody else lined up in the aisle, their thoughts on prayer and God, and the corners of their eyes riveted on me remaining in the pew like I had another wife someplace. Rather than suffer through such moments, I would say a prayer that I was truly sorry and get on line with the rest.

Suddenly I could not afford to continue this private faith. If this whole thing turned into something real, which of course it would not because there was nothing wrong with me, but even on the faintest chance that something could be wrong, then the soul was not the part of me that could wait until I felt ready to take care of it. Now it must be an equal to the body. For you cannot live with temporal danger and ignore the eternal.

There is no such thing as an ex-Catholic. At the start, you have no choice nor do you even know where you are or what they are doing. But once they put water on your head and an adult speaks for you, you are a Catholic for all the days through all the years until they pray over your grave.

You can fall away from the religion as long as you please, for years, for decades; you can deny it through a thousand cock crows, you can luxuriate in sin. But let there be one sharp chest pain, one deep moment of dizziness, and that is some loud bawl that you let out for a priest.

Perhaps the ambulance crew can save your life, but for sure the priest saves your eternity.

The Catholic Church is held together by one word: *calamity*.

I'll tell you where I learned that best. Jacqueline Kennedy is in the waiting room outside of emergency room one, Parkland Hospital, where her husband was dead, and she was talking earnestly to the priest who had just given her husband the last rites of the church. She nodded numbly and the priest touched her arm and left.

The priest's name was Oscar Huber, and I found him that evening in the rectory of Holy Trinity Church, a handsome brick building in the Oaklawn area. It is about two and a half miles from the hospital.

"Mrs. Kennedy asked me if this was a valid last rites," he said quietly. "I assured her that it was. The church law is that there is about two hours from the time that death is pronounced and the soul departs from the body. If you administer the last rites during that period, it is a valid last sacrament. I anointed the president about an hour after he had been brought to the hospital. This was well within the two-hour period. I assured Mrs. Kennedy of this and she said, Thank you. She was relieved."

And so here I was flinging open the church doors and looking for that white light over the confessional booth to indicate that the Franciscan Order, which runs the church, had a man in there working on sin. I said a prayer and walked to the confessional. Here in the white light was the name. "Father Mychal Judge."

This sent me straight backward. I know Mychal Judge so well and for so long that there could be no way for me to get in there and try the usual higher voice tone delivered through a hand held to the mouth. I slid into a pew and attended 6:15 P.M. mass. At the end of which I looked up in hopes a new priest would be on confession duty. Judge still had his shingle out.

I looked at the altar and said, "Put me down for trying. I'll make it next time."

In the morning the doctor giving the angiogram, Berenstein, said to me, "Now you know what we are doing?"

"Sure, it's nothing," I said.

"We are going to do an angiogram to see if that is an aneurysm in the front of your brain or not."

He repeated once more that some of the doctors at the weekly neurological meeting thought that the suspicious formation in the front of my brain, right between the two hemispheres, could be an aneurysm. It had absolutely nothing to do with the trouble in my left eye. Berenstein said that some others thought that the bulge was innocuous.

"What do you think?" I asked him.

He answered by being busy.

He did say that the aneurysm was the smallest lesion in the human body that kills. Which is why I was here for this angiogram, whose sight is even more penetrating and revealing than an MRI's. I was on this table under lights in the radiology department on the second floor of the hospital. Of course I was certain that an angiogram consisted of attaching wires to my body and conducting an unseen, secret electrical test. Afterward, the doctors would stare at computer terminals and proclaim that I had done wonderfully, that there was nothing in the world the matter with me, that I should go out for a good big breakfast.

But in the reality of morning in November in the hospital, Berenstein explained that they were going to cut into my right leg at the groin and insert a plastic catheter of three millimeters into the large artery. He said that by guiding the catheter by wire they would run it straight up the artery, crossing the chest, and then up to the inside of my head. What would it do there? It would shoot dye that gives a marked contrast into my whole head, all over the brain, and it would provide the contrast for all the pictures they would be shooting. This is how the angiogram gives the clearest look at blood vessels. I felt this was an inhuman manner in which to treat me. Here I never had been in a hospital before, except to visit others, and yet in my very first hour they were putting me into a stakes race: they were cutting into an artery.

Berenstein said to me, "I understand that you do some sort of journalism work." He touched the middle of my forehead, just above the eyes. "This bulge we're looking at is right near the parts of your brain that give you the cognitive skills that you use for writing. We'll have to be very careful with you."

He did not tell me what he was thinking about. There had been a priest who didn't take kindly to an angiogram and the parts of the priest's brain that gave him emotions were damaged and no matter what people said or did around him, no matter what they confessed or requested, he felt nothing.

If I knew that, and also the origins of this test, I would have been in an intense debate with myself as to whether to leave the building naked to hail a cab or take the time to get my clothes. The angiogram was developed by Egas Moniz of Portugal. He eventually won a Nobel Prize for it but the patients did not. On his way to world fame, Moniz killed quite a few people with his early angiograms. Around the year 1939, his peers began saying to Moniz, "Why not try it out on animals?" Moniz said of course not and forged ahead. Therefore in the mornings wide eyes stared up from the table as Moniz stomped around with his catheter. When he inserted it into the artery and ran it up to the brain, sometimes the wide eyes turned into stones. And Moniz would be asked once more, "Why not try it out on animals?"

Now, suddenly on this morning of my angiogram, Berenstein the doctor was gone and there were men and women in green-blue operating room clothes around me and my right thigh was numb. I thought I could feel somebody using something to cut into the groin. Hands were pushing down hard on the groin and for sure I felt something being stuffed into my leg. I closed my eyes and tried to fall asleep. For one of the few times in my life, I could not.

After about twenty minutes of intermittent humming, in which there were these buzzes of pictures being taken somewhere, a voice over a speaker said, "We're going to place some liquid through the catheter. You will feel your head getting warm from it. We need it to give us contrast for the pictures. Now you might see a few sparks behind your eyes. Don't worry about it."

In a control room they were taking sequential pictures of my blood vessels at the rate of two and three pictures per second.

A dishpan of hot water splashed inside

my head. There was a series of lightning streaks behind both eyes.

This dye swirling around the brain can put you into major shock, but nobody had made a point of this, and therefore, not knowing, I had nothing to fear.

One of the people hovering over the table, a tall guy, was gone and then he came back.

"We're doing well," he said.

"What's it look like so far?" I asked.

"You have an aneurysm. We just have to make sure it's the only one. You know, between sixteen and twenty percent of people with an aneurysm have more than one."

I looked around and saw my friend Norman Wikler, the doctor. "Norman, I just blew a photo." He seemed distressed, and also amazed at my lack of understanding of what it all meant. What it meant was that I was in a lot of trouble, but that I also was treating it just as I do any horrible thing that occurs in a day. I report on a tragedy by remaining cold and callous and concentrate on making notes of the smallest details. In the hotel kitchen in Los Angeles, I counted Sirhan Sirhan kicking his legs five times before somebody sat on them after he shot Robert Kennedy. By remaining that distant, I can write an account without nerves interfering. I go home and sleep beautifully. When it hits, about dawn, I am up and I am sick.

I now had to stay on my back in a recovery room for five hours because they had cut a hole in a major artery, like the biggest I have, and it needed time to close up. If it did not close up, I would close down.

I had nothing, not even a drip of water, and now I asked the nurse if I could have coffee and she brought me some and it was instant and vile and I complained and she said that was all there was until the lunch was brought in. That would be soon, she said.

So I was in this empty room, but with so many monitors around the bed that I couldn't see the other side of the room and had to strain to see anything on my side. The monitors around my bed would go unused. But they sure were needed elsewhere, for the room did not remain empty.

Now there was a great rattle at the double doors to the room and I knew of course that this was the cart coming from the kitchen and I strained to see it arrive.

The doors flew open and in stormed a gurney with a guy on it whose toes were straight up and who had so many intravenous bottles and plastic bags hanging over him that it appeared his life was hanging by

90

the thinnest thread at this very moment. The immediate sight of a doctor walking quickly after him seemed to confirm the doubtfulness. Right off, the doctor was calling, "Mister Rocklein! Wake up Mister Rocklein! Your operation is over!"

To my surprise, the man in bed stirred so slightly. "Aggghhhh."

"You're going to be fine, Mister Rocklein," the doctor said.

There was another rattle and the door opened again. I could taste a piece of bread with coffee. Instead here came another body rattling through the doorway, bottles rocking, doctor following.

What I was catching was the end of the morning surgery run, which was the same as the aftermath of a bombing raid. Here they came, one after the other. I am looking for coffee and eggs and they are giving me cut stomachs. They were being pushed by male orderlies who with their bare arms looked like they were shoving a cart through a warehouse. Each time a doctor followed calling out, "Wake up!" So far, everybody that I saw or heard did seem to wake up.

The next sound was of a rolling bed that was put into the next clearing from me. A doctor hurried in.

"Wake up, Sam."

Who did not move.

"Sam. Wake up. Your operation is through."

Sam was inert.

"Sam!"

Now the doctor bent over him. "Is he breathing?" he said to the nurse.

She put her head down and said nothing.

"Sam!" the doctor called.

As success was somewhat reluctant to make itself known, the doctor gave a slight display of uncertainty.

"Is he breathing?"

"I don't know," the nurse said. "I'll get a mirror."

The doctor let out a yelp. "SAM!"

The nurse had her ear right up against Sam's nose. Then she straightened triumphantly.

"This time he's breathing."

Which meant the last time he was not. The realization of this, and how close it all had been, had the doctor's knees buckling.

I asked the nurse at my bed, "What is the matter with Sam?"

"Either a heart bypass or a brain tumor. A brain tumor, I think I heard them say." From where we were she couldn't see if he had a chest wound or a wrapped-up head.

"Beautiful," I told her.

When they finally let me up five hours later, the tall thin guy from the test looked out of an office and handed me a large brown envelope with a copy of my angiogram film. It appeared to be a map of rivers and tributaries.

"What do I do with this?" I asked him.

"Show them to your neurosurgeon. If you're smart, you'll get this operated on right away."

He took a pen and wrote down a name on the corner of the envelope. "If you look at other places, this is one we all know." He wrote down, "Spetzler. Phoenix."

When I came into the waiting room, my wife appeared nonchalant. "Well, you're certainly lucky."

"I'm sorry."

"Sorry? You ought to go to one of your churches and pray."

"Why?"

"Why? Because you could die. You found out about this before anything happened. And by sheer luck."

On the way home, I got out of the car at Fifth Avenue and 55th Street and walked along the street for several minutes to see for myself what kind of people were out shopping. I needed this scene for the end of the column I told you about. I now had four hours to get it in. I went home and finished the column, which was about the country having official classes, the same as the British. There is the high class, which is not an issue because there are so few in it. Then there is the middle class, which is an official class as everybody learned from the elections. But if you were not middle class, then what were you? You were low class. And you were low class because that is exactly what you were: low class. Which was why I checked Fifth Avenue: to see how many low-class people were obstructing the street in the gold evening light of the stores. The low class must be run off the better streets because low-class people cannot even walk properly. They trudge along, bumping, swaying, starting one way and going another. At all times they get in the way of the proper people, the high class and the middle class, who walk with body control and confident, even footstrike. Writing this that night, I advocated buyouts for the poor on welfare with the payments predicated on their leaving the city. The column was done at home and sent by fax to the office before 9:00 P.M. I went to bed and passed out with the angiogram film next to my side of the bed. I woke up at 6:00 A.M. with my eye staring at the name written in pen on the bottom corner of the envelope: Spetzler, Phoenix.

That's pretty good. But I wasn't going out and have my head opened up like a car hood on the strength of one message on an envelope.

I made coffee in the kitchen and called Burt Roberts before he called me. He is the chief judge in the Bronx County, which is like colonials presiding over the whole Caribbean. We speak on the phone every morning at seven, provided we are talking, and have been doing this for a century, or since the time Roberts called me at my newspaper office and introduced himself. "Hiya kid. Red Roberts. I work in Hogan's office." Frank Hogan was the Manhattan district attorney. "Look. I'm going someplace and you're going someplace. We ought to get together."

I could still hear him saying this. Once, I read somewhere that a man is fortunate if he can meet even the shadow of a friend. Roberts's stone honesty, intellect, and uninhibited personality made him one of the half-dozen personalities of his city of his time. No question. He also had such a fear of being off a municipal payroll, and the attendant pension, that he never took the chance to run for some bigger office. So in his years people half his size became mayor while he remained at home and put up a grotto for his pension papers. But he had a way of replacing the adulation from crowds, and that was to concentrate totally on the sound of his own voice.

Now, I walked out onto the cold terrace with the phone and stood in the dead yellow-green of a lot of plants dead for the winter and looked toward his building, over on Second Avenue.

"I'm going to have a brain operation," I said.

"It's really great, isn't it?" he said.

"Not so good when they have to take my head off."

"Yeah, it's great. You work like I do, work like a dog, and I have to go to the hospital today. Isn't that something?"

"Because of your leg?" I asked him.

"That was my ribs, you putz. That was last summer. It's my chin this time. I told you the chin. I got a mole on it."

"I guess I forgot. I've had my own troubles. They're going to open up my head to the bra—"

"— I go in for all the preliminary exams today. You know something? You know what kills people? Ego. When I used to play ball I never wore a hat. I wanted people to

96

see that head of red hair. Now look at me. Because of all that sun they want me in the hospital. It's only a little thing on my chin, but they want it to come off. Ach. What a pain."

"I guess I'll be out for a few days myself," I said.

"Why?"

"Because I'm having a brain operation."

"Well, it's really great. I'm working day and night on the Happy Land fire. Eighty-seven dead. That's eighty-seven cases I'm trying to settle. First I'm the judge at the criminal trial. After that, I have to settle the damages. Ach. What do I get for it? I go to the hospital this morning. It's great, isn't it? Really great."

Which is how Roberts will remember all this. The time he had a mole on his chin.

Roberts was the model for the judge character in Tom Wolfe's *Bonfire of the Vanities*. I have to live with the guy and Wolfie counts the money.

I hang up and look at the start of a winter morning from the cold terrace of our apartment. The sky is wide cold pink near rose spreading over the last high gray wall of night. The stone buildings are still dark and the early people walk with shoulders hunched and hands in overcoat pockets. On the street below me, light from the corner fruit market burns a circle into the darkness. I could have looked at about five thousand things better than this, too. Because suddenly I am remembering a chiaroscuro I was raised on, the one bare bulb over the gas station door a few yards across the side street on 101st Avenue. On my knees with my arms folded on the bedroom windowsill, watching the street for someone to come home, my uncle; the father was well gone and running. I waited like this for long hours each night until the bare light bulb went off and old Tomasullo shut up the gas station for the night. When he did that, I went to bed feeling sorry for myself.

Here now I see in my mind the young woman in the front room of her dim first-floor apartment on St. John's Place in a part of Brooklyn where everything is torn. It is January. Her name is Bernice Simmons and she does not know where she is, really, and when she smiles it was the same as looking up at one of these military trucks in Vietnam where all the women were riding with the bodies of their sons or husbands and when you looked at them they smiled and even giggled against the pain piercing them.

"I don't know what I'm going to do with this, there is so much room." Bernice Simmons is tall and young, twenty-three, and wearing a red plaid shirt and jeans. She is showing her new apartment. She walks around the bare room with walls dark with the years of soot. "I guess I can put a couch over here." She points to a wall. "But it's so dark." She walked across the bare dusty soot-stained floors to a scarred door that opened into a deep closet.

The closet would have given her room for toys and clothes of her three children, ages three, two and one. They had been in foster care while social workers helped the mother find this apartment. The children were in bed in the basement of their foster home in the Bronx, the other cold January night, protected from prowlers by a refrigerator wedged against the basement door. When the fire in the back of the basement started, the woman in the house could not move the refrigerator and when people from the street tried to break in through the basement door, they could not budge it, either. So the three children, ages three, two and one, died in the smoke and flames. A social worker came around to see the mother in her bare new dusty apartment and told her that all her kids were dead.

Now she stood in the closet doorway. "My knee-highs gone," she said.

Inside on the floor was a large cardboard box with a little blue sweater showing at the top. From the box came the thick sour smell of fire.

There was sudden pain in remembering this. So I let my eyes go up the block to the winter green of Central Park, set off with bare gray-violet trees. Beyond the park are the buildings of the East Side, graceful stone buildings of twelve stories. They were put up well before the modern political system ruined architecture by taking money for expensive campaigns and giving in return the right to spoil the sky for all to see for the hideous glass towers with flat roofs that climb fifty and sixty stories. Beyond the buildings, there rise the three old gray iron towers that end in gray speartips piercing the sky to announce the presence of the Queensboro Bridge. From each tower there slope and then climb the graceful cables holding up the bridge. Underneath the bridge, unseen from my terrace but certainly there, are the swift waters of the East River. Beyond the bridge in the darkness there are the roofs of Queens, a tar meadow that runs to the horizon without showing an interesting feature. And somewhere at the end of this horizon, the ocean.

Of course on a morning like this I envisioned my tidal wave, moving across the land, dripping thick white foam at the top and the bottom yanking the earth to bits. I hear a great crack and the fifty-seven-story building next to mine wraps its arms around its middle and drops straight down, as if going feet first off a cliff. The gray towers of the bridge disappear. Pilings that support thousands of tons and are driven into the river water through the silt and down to the cold, dark rock bottom, suddenly dissolve. The bridge falls into the river, which covers it with gray fast waters as if nothing had happened and it really had not.

Now into the light on the street below steps a form whose size cannot be judged but the color of the red T-shirt worn in the winter cold says that it is Angelo from the Elite coffee shop. He stands there smoking a cigarette, which he must do no matter how cold the air. He can't smoke inside the place. He talks to a man in an apron who sits in front of the fruit stand. Suddenly the man's arm rises and falls. He is chopping something on a table in front of him. He is chopping it with a machete, I guess, and doing it right in front of me. Here comes the machete blade out of the shadows and into the light, starting high up and coming down on something, what is it? it has to be a coconut on a table. He is chopping the head off a freaking coconut. The top of the coconut goes off. I feel the top of my head coming off. This is what they are going to do to me, I remind myself.

I went inside and tried to forget the whole thing. Which I cannot. I waited until nine and then started calling. I already had been given the name of a surgeon in New York and the first thing I did was call an old friend, Dr. Saul Farber, the head of New York University Medical School. He is considered a giant of his time in his city.

When I mentioned the name of the neurosurgeon I had been told about, Farber said, "You only have one brain."

He comes out of Borough Park in Brooklyn and he went to New Utrecht High School. How else is he supposed to talk to me?

"Get it operated on," he said. "The aneurysm is in a perfect spot to be removed. And it is in a perfect spot to cause the most damage if it bursts."

"Where should I go?" I asked.

Farber told me, "Spetzler in Phoenix has done the most aneurysms. You might as well take advantage of all that experience."

"When should I look to get it done?" I am thinking of three or four months. When

I am good and ready, I told myself.

"Try and go down there today," Farber said. "I'll call him."

It turned out that Spetzler was away and I was asked to send the film. I walked to the Federal Express at 79th and Broadway, where you usually see people sending out overdue movie scripts to the West Coast. I told the clerk, "This is my *Gone With the Wind*."

When I walked back, I stopped at the candy store next to the Regency Theater on Broadway and 67th to buy a paper. The little Arab behind the counter was talking on a hand phone and at the same time making change for me. Next to me was a tall kid, a messenger, with a sack on his back. He has his bike right inside the door and he is buying a candy bar. The Arab keeps talking.

"Who are you talking to?" I asked him.

"Yemen," he said. He continued talking on the phone. It also happened to be the truth. The city may be thrashing, but it still is the only place in the world where people make a phone call to Yemen from a candy store.

"What's the weather like?"

He talked in the phone and said, "Not so cold as here."

"Is he near the desert?"

He nodded yes and kept talking.

"All over the world," the messenger says.

We left together and he picked up his bike and walked it along the sidewalk. Just to show interest, I asked him where he was going. He took a package out of the sack on his back and looked at it. The address was Associated Booking Corp., 1995 Broadway. It was only a few doors up. "Oh, I know the place," I said.

Of course anything I looked at now made me think of something bad. I'm sorry, but I am not used to having a brain operation on my mind.

It was in the offices of Associated Booking that I ran into a cheap villain whose life as we know it was sired by another cheap villain, Oswald, and they caused the country the most trouble of my time and they were the least of all people.

Ruby. I am in the Associated offices when Joe Glazer owned the outfit. The office at that time was over on West 57th. Joe Glazer was a lord of entertainment, the agent for people like Louis Armstrong and Barbra Streisand. I was hanging around his office because he also managed Sugar Ray Robinson and I wanted to hear him tell me that he was pulling Robinson out. Robinson couldn't fight a little bit anymore, but he refused to quit. Joe Glazer was out of Chicago, and was as tough as a steer. He spoke profanities in a rasping voice. He had a sharp nose and gray hair slicked straight back and wore expensive gray suits and white socks that sagged.

Joe Glazer said to me, "Say hello to my dear friend Jack Ruby."

"Hello. Where you from?"

"Dallas, I got a big nightclub."

"The greatest!" Glazer said. Ruby owned a strip joint one flight up from some street in Dallas.

"Can I talk?" Ruby said, indicating me.

"Sure, say whatever you effin' please," Glazer said.

"Joe, I'm rebuilding my whole joint."

"Great! I want you to see somethin'." Joe jumped up and led us out of the office and down a hall to his mail room. There, he patted a new Pitney Bowes stamp machine as if he were sending it out for the Preakness.

"This is the greatest machine in the world," Glazer said. "Nobody has one like it. They just built it for me. It does everything. It even seals the envelopes."

He went back to his desk and began licking envelopes. After that, he licked loose stamps and pounded them onto the envelopes. He took a stack of these letters and sat on them like an old hen.

"Why don't you use the machine?" Ruby asked.

"Because I don't use it," Glazer said.

Ruby changed the subject to what he was in the place for. "Joe, my new place is going to sit a thousand."

"Great!" Glazer said.

"I got to open big. I need Louis."

"You got him!" Glazer said. He shouted, "Miss Church! Get me Louis right away."

Soon onto the speaker phone came the voice of Louis Armstrong. "Daddy, Daddy, I love you."

"Louis. I got Jack Ruby here."

Armstrong answered by breathing.

"Jack as you know is one of our dearest friends. The dearest! Jack is opening the biggest effin' place in Texas and we're goin' in and open it up for him."

"As good as Swiss Kriss," Louis said.

Jack Ruby was just about sobbing when he leaned over Glazer's desk and called into the speaker: "Louis. How can I ever thank you."

"Pay my daddy Joe."

"There is no price," Ruby said. "Joe decides."

Louis called to Glazer, "Daddy, since we talkin', send me five thousand today."

Jack Ruby, holding his hat, bowing and scraping to Glazer, left. Of course nobody heard from him again.

Until the next year when he came into Joe Glazer's office and said he was opening a huge new showplace in Dallas and he could not open with anybody less than Ella.

"You got her! Miss Church, get Ella on the phone."

Now on the speaker came the voice of Ella Fitzgerald.

"Ella, I got Jack Ruby here."

"You got who?"

"Jack Ruby. He's our dearest friend in Dallas. Write the date down. April. We're opening his big huge new nightclub."

And Ruby went away. A year later, I met Glazer at the Hickory House on 52nd Street and he hollered from his table, "Where were you? Jack Ruby was in today. He wants Lionel Hampton for his new joint."

Now I was here on Broadway in New York with a bike messenger and in the midst of remembering these things I had this stray thought: Was I going to be able to do this afterward? Was I going to be able to walk around and, on the odd instant, remember things out of my life? Stop it, I told myself.

You'll just go into the hospital in the spring and get this thing over with and it'll be done and gone. I was still thinking I had all the time I wanted.

That was all I told myself, too. Because it was too big to begin to calculate.

Later, I met Peter Johnson and a friend of his, Dr. Richard Bergland, then the chairman of the neurosurgery department of Beth Israel Hospital in Manhattan. Bergland took a duplicate of my angiogram out of the envelope and held it up to the light. We were in Veniero's, an Italian coffee and pastry shop on East 11th Street. I sat with my wife. The film in Bergland's hands showed the dark lines of blood vessels in a circle. In the middle of which was the small black bulge of an aneurysm. Yes, the film showed the river with tributaries as I first saw, but now after a half-dozen doctors hanging the film on a wall and lecturing about it, I had an idea of what it was about. For on the right side of the picture was a spiderweb of lines. But the left side was a total blank. This was because the left side of the circuit of blood vessels was not there. As the report in my hand said, "The anterior Circle of Willis shows a minor anomaly with no visualization of the left A1 and appearance of both A2's filling in from the right." There was nothing on the left. Everybody had said this was nothing to worry about. The construction of the blood system in my brain did not conform with the line drawings or pictures from a textbook, but this was the way it is with almost all people. Nobody has vessels supplying the brain that follow form. What it means in my case, however, is that the unusual was more pronounced. The main blood vessel coming up from the major artery, the carotid artery, became the tube, which on film looked like a water pipe, coming up the right side. There was no tube on the left. In from the right was the anterior communicating artery that connected the right vessels to the left. The aneurysm was in the exact middle of the anterior communicating artery. It blocked nothing. It was a bulge on an artery. It resembled a bubble on a tire tube. The single solitary most dangerous bubble you'll ever see. "I don't like it at all," Bergland said.

"They told me it was small," I said.

"It is about six millimeters and you go a little bit over that and it is the right size to burst. See this little nipple on the end of it? I don't like that at all."

"Where do you think I should go?" I said.

"Spetzler. Nobody else in the world."

I told him that I already had sent film

and that Spetzler wouldn't be at his office in Phoenix until Tuesday of the next week.

"Can you get a plane to Phoenix this afternoon? Be there anyway on the chance he comes back early," Bergland said.

"There's nobody right here in New York or Boston?" I asked.

"They do forty to fifty aneurysms at Columbia Presbyterian but with residents, they have thirty neurosurgeons up there. You can't have one doing all the aneurysms. So nobody does the fifty. I was at Mass General and they had thirty-six surgeons. You couldn't have one guy do everything. So nobody became experienced enough at anything. In the whole country, you have four thousand neurosurgeons and only seven thousand fresh primary malignant brain tumors a year. And nobody here does many aneurysms. Spetzler has done thousands. You go to the man who does the most."

Right away, I told him that the doctor at NYU, Berenstein, who had done the angiogram on me, had a system in which he did the same invasion as with an angiogram, but then shot metal pellets through the catheter and into the aneurysm. The pellets were magnesium and upon coming out of the catheter, they twirled up into coils. He said it was the future of brain surgery. Put away the knife and go with his coils. It sounded beautiful. Now I asked Bergland, "If the aneurysm is so weak that it's liable to burst on its own, how can it hold any metal in it?" He said the magnesium caused the blood to coagulate. And he really doesn't have to open up my head? When he told me no, I was elated.

"What if it doesn't work?" Bergland said. "That can happen."

"I always can have an operation, right?" I said.

"That is too much risk, one procedure after another. Berenstein is a genius but not for you this time. Someday, it is going to be the thing of the future. Maybe in five years. Right now, just go to Spetzler."

He asked me, "What do you do during the day?"

"I'm going to work and then I go home and swim."

"You can forget the swimming," he said. "You can't put any pressure on the artery. The first thing you do is buy some stool softener. Most aneurysms burst when you're pressing yourself on the toilet. The same for sex. You can't have sexual relations."

He looked right at my wife, too. She could do without a strange man talking about bathroom and sex to her. But I

111

thought right away of Miguelito, a skinny little man who sang at the Chib Chah on Roosevelt Avenue in Jackson Heights. The room was filled with cocaine and large guns. He dropped dead one night at home. Miguelito's wife told my friend Ramona Torres that he had died during sex with her. "He got up with this worst headache. He got nothing to say. He falls on the floor. Boom. Dead. No time even for good-bye."

"The cocaine," Ramona said.

"No, no cocaine. They cut him all open and found he had an anyeur."

I didn't know what that was. But I sure could spell it for her now.

I believed implicitly in what Bergland was telling me. I immediately went to the East Side to another doctor, an old friend, with credentials that reach across oceans. He said he didn't see why I was racing so frantically for an operation. He said there was a one to three percent chance in any year that an aneurysm would burst. But that there was a ten percent chance of something going wrong in an operation, from outright death to coming out of it unable to tell time. You put the ten percent risk in an operation together with the ten percent risk of an angiogram, which I would have almost immediately after the operation so they could make sure it worked out, and you are at twenty percent. As I already had one angiogram, perhaps I had a parting of the ways with even the most thoughtful of medical statistical-gathering. I now was as open as an archway for unavoidable error, or vessels that become weary from being plucked and probed, or for the unknown that leaves you forever short of full consciousness.

By doing nothing, I had this one to three percent chance. As I was talking to the doctor, I smelled the sea air at Bantry in Ireland. Oh, that is exactly where I would go, gambling each day with my life by myself, sparing all family involved if the result suddenly came up bad and I got beat by something with only a three point chance. All risk would be taken in a place where those in the town square could care less if you lost and dropped dead right in front of them. They would have no trouble in simply pitching me into the bay, which is the longest, deepest and coldest bay in all of Europe.

Once, the old retired undertaker in Bantry told me about his greatest day in the funeral business, which was when the *Lusitania* was struck by a torpedo and went under just a short distance offshore at Kinsale. "The water was covered with t'ousands of bodies," he said. "It was marvelous."

In my time he sat on the bench in front of the Anchor Tavern in Bantry, just sitting in the sun before the rain, when a French supertanker blew up out in Bantry Bay. Right away, the old undertaker hollered for Patty Minihane, who owned the clothing shop on the square. Patty counted the bodies, seventy-two, rushed off by car to his Cork City wholesaler and returned with expensive suits, although not as expensive as they would be when his pencil hit the pad, and pairs of new shoes to dress the seventy-two French Catholics for their funerals.

And as I was talking to the doctor friend of mine, I didn't think the notion of gambling with my life in Bantry was such a careless thought. Rather, I was absolutely convinced that it was a great joining of common sense and science. I can continue living and if anything ends that, then, no bother, simply pitch the remains into this deep bay. Immediately this lifted the heavy dread of having my head opened. Just as suddenly, a most ominous thought rose through the elation. If I had a one to three percent chance of dropping dead in one year, did that mean that at the end of the year I could be alive and great but that the odds suddenly would be drawn to two to six percent? And in the third year they would be three to nine percent? I reminded myself that of course this couldn't be true, that I was merely looking at the bleak side of a subject.

I said to the doctor, "About this one to three percent chance in any year. Of course that means that at the end of the year we start all over again and it is one to three percent in the next year."

"Actually, no."

"You mean that you add it to next year?"

"Yes."

"So the one to three percent suddenly means a two to six percent."

"Maybe."

"What if I've had this thing inside me for thirty years? I could be a ninety percent risk right now."

"It doesn't appear to be so dangerously large," he said. Which was not enough for me. Already I had been told, and believed, that the aneurysm was the smallest lesion in the body that can kill. Now I am being told that it isn't such a big lesion. I'll stay with the most troublesome opinion. If the guy is wrong and it isn't anything at all, what do I do, sue?

When I thought about it, I realized that the doctor was not in neurosurgery. I used to think that all very smart doctors knew about every area whether they worked in it or not. But now I thought of how Nelson Rockefeller used a doctor named Esakof, who lived down the block from me in Queens. Esakof was an oncologist, a cancer doctor, and Rockefeller had a cardiac problem. Which is how he went: wine, women and cardiac.

Therefore, I would take no opinion from an oncologist, even a friend of mine, about an aneurysm. With it, any notion of gambling to duck an operation was gone.

When Nelson Rockefeller, with all his hundreds of millions, his houses, his titles, went down dead on the floor of one of his houses on 54th Street in Manhattan, the Rockefeller employees started out that night by saying that he had died in his office in Rockefeller Center. That didn't make much sense as it was late on a Friday night. I am outside LaScala Restaurant with my friend Dick Oliver from the *Daily News* newspaper, and here is an Emergency Medical Service ambulance standing in traffic. The driver, whom I knew from the Eastern Queens YMCA, looked out the window and said, "Hey, we got Rocky down on West 54th."

Later, another ambulance driver said he had picked up the body in a town house on West 54th Street. He said the young woman involved fled down the street. Somebody else placed her in the ambulance. But all this lying by Rockefeller's people already had started lightning streaks of gossip, the most accepted being that Henry Kissinger, a family retainer, had been in an orgy with Rockefeller and the woman. Certainly, it was absolutely wrong. But you lie, and somebody else lies right back.

I had been booked onto *The Tonight Show* for November 22 and when I called Paul Raehpour from the show and said I couldn't make it, he said, Well, why don't we try the next night?

"I can't. I have a little thing with an eye doctor."

"It's not serious?"

"Oh, of course not. How could it be serious if it involves me? I'll be back in three days."

In our family we had young people who lived on computers, two of them working as producers at networks and another with good newspaper training, and each day they searched the medical files on computers and brought home piles of printouts on neurosurgery. The others asked anybody they knew. Soon it became apparent that you could fit all the good brain surgeons in the last row of a movie house. We made up a list as you would when doing something in politics. We had twenty names of surgeons on it and then we began to go to them one by one and ask them how they would vote.

Each day there was a high pile of things to read. Some days it wasn't all that technical. Insanity never is.

I have a friend named Dick Blood, who worked with me at the *Daily News* and who then went to teach at Columbia Journalism School. He called and said he had a story from the *Baltimore Evening Sun* that in 1979 won the first Pulitzer for feature writing. "It's an aneurysm operation," he said. Did I want to see it? Why, certainly, send it, Dick. And he did and this is what it said:

In the cold hours of a winter morning, Dr. Thomas Barbee Ducker, chief brain surgeon at the University of Maryland Hospital, rises before dawn. His wife serves him waffles, but no coffee. Coffee makes his hands shake.

In downtown Baltimore, on the 12th floor of University Hospital, Edna Kelly's husband tells her good-bye. For 57 years Mrs. Kelly shared her skull with a monster: No more. Today she is frightened but determined.

It is 6:30 A.M.

"I'm not afraid to die," she said as

this day approached. . . .

Beautiful. I don't even want to look. I go to the end, which I figured had to be good news:

"That should be the aneurysm right there," says Dr. Ducker. "Why the hell can't we get to it? We've tried, ten times."

. . . Already, where the monster's tentacles hang before the brainstem, the tissue swells, pinching off the source of oxygen.

Mrs. Kelly is dying.

The clock on the wall, near where Dr. Ducker sits, says 1:40.

Blood calls a day later. "How did you like it?" I couldn't talk. How did I like it? How did I like what he did? How do you like sending me a thing like that?

Then Emily Eldridge found one book about Robert Spetzler, written by Ed Sylvester of Arizona State University. I was dazed from all the dangers that were mentioned, and I glanced at one page that said: "Setting a Yasergil aneurysm clip, for example, requires the surgeon to hold a pair of long-handled pliers in one hand, six inches or more above the small aneurysm deep in the cavity he has created. He has to be steady enough to keep the far end of this wand, which holds the clip open, from wavering. Then, from this height, he must rotate the wrist clockwise or counterclockwise until the clip aligns with the ballooned-out artery. When the alignment is just so, gently release, and the clip closes down, sealing the balloon off from the still-firm vascular tubing. And if that position is not 'just so,' then the clip must be reseated in the pliers' nose, opened wide, tried again."

Pliers in my head. I put that book down and that was the end of that reading. I knew in there somewhere was a description of how they get through the skull to work on the brain. They would break into my head like it was a store. I didn't want to read a line about that.

We kept our voting list on the neurosurgeons. Of the twenty votes we got, only one did not list Robert Spetzler as at least co-first choice, with himself. Most put Spetzler alone. Before he left his job due to inclement voting, Mario Cuomo asked the state health commissioner, Mark Chassin, to make a recommendation for my case. Chassin took the place of David Axelrod, who had an aneurysm burst and who spent three years unconscious on a respirator without the flicker of an eye to indicate life. Axelrod had devoted so much time to pushing for a Living Will in the state. After he collapsed, his family would not take him off the respirator. His years of reasoned, intelligent advocacy dissolved in the fear and grief of a family at a bedside. For my case, Chassin put in a full day asking about doctors, after which he reported, "There are three surgeons in New York who can do this operation very well. However, if there is anything unusual, I would go to Spetzler."

Cuomo said, "I think Breslin feels that it is a very unusual aneurysm. It is in HIS brain."

By now, I was having these random, but surprisingly casual thoughts about dying, or much worse, turning into a turnip that requires nursing.

The idea of my dying was fascinating to me. No, it did not frighten me. From the start, in this small experience, the fear almost always was absent and this is something that we will examine carefully as we get closer to those hours when you have a right to be scared out of breath. Right now, I simply wonder what happens when I die. I sure had been around it before. My first wife, Rosemary, died fourteen years ago. We lived together in love and affection that was deeper when she died in the middle of a rainy night in June in 1981 than when I met her on a Saturday night in the spring of 1952. She came running into the Crossroads Bar, right on the corner from my first newspaper, the *Long Island Press*. There were two other girls in gowns, and guys in tuxedos, running excitedly in the rain. The car had dropped dead across the street on the way home from the wedding.

She came through the door laughing and with rain on her face. She was in a long peach gown and held the wedding bouquet she had caught. She looked right at me.

"I caught the bride's bouquet," she said.

She threw the flowers to me.

"Now you caught it. You want to get married?"

"Who to?"

"Me."

"Sure."

The others came spinning through the door like gaily colored pinwheels, but the two of us stood and talked only to each other.

When she had to leave, she wrote down her name and phone number on a beer coaster. Then she was gone. She was halfway up the El steps outside the bar when she crouched down and looked through the spokes and waved to me.

We were married in 1954 at St. Pancras Church in Glendale on a cold December morning.

I knew she was gone just as fast as I fell in love with her. She had an operation for breast cancer in 1976 and then seemed fine for years. But then she was not feeling well and we had a yearly checkup date anyway so we were up at the Dana-Farber Cancer Institute in Boston and I bought *Time* and *Newsweek,* which both had the same cover, about whether there was a hidden mother in Heaven because God had a son. The editors get scared and steal from each other. I began getting good and edgy. Rosemary came back from one test and said we had to wait. The doctor came out and said, "We just want her for one more test. They dropped a slide."

He smiled easily and Rosemary went with him and I put those magazines down and I sat on the edge of the chair with the roots of my hair cold with fright. When she came back holding a small patch of cotton on the inside of her elbow, I saw that doctor in the hall and I went right behind him, and he didn't hear me coming because I know how to walk down a hallway when I want something, and he goes into this bright laboratory room and says to a dark-faced woman with a dot on her face, an Indian from India, "Could you do this again? I just want to be certain."

I knew that no slide had been dropped. I went back to Rosemary and wanted to take her hand right away, but I thought that would make her think that something was wrong. So I sat and tried to talk. It was hard. She was cheerful and I was afraid.

I don't know how long it was, but the doctor came walking back quickly. "We have a problem," he said. He led the way to a small office. "There is something wrong with an enzyme test."

I always thought enzymes were in your saliva. Sitting at his gunmetal gray desk with one folder on it, with only a couple of sheets in the folder, he said, "There is a test that I didn't like. I had them do it again. There is a problem with your liver."

His phone rang and I didn't look at Rosemary because I was too busy reading the sheet in front of him on his desk. Always that was my hidden strength. I could read anything upside down and backward. This time I read the word *metastasize*.

After which I never heard the guy when

he began talking.

I knew the word *metastasize* from the night at the *Long Island Press* newspaper when Fred McMorrow, reading copy, suddenly sat bolt upright. "Imbecile!" He spun and glared at some poor guy who had been given some hospital story and the field was not quite his. McMorrow roared, " 'By moving through the body it caused it to metastasize.' Moron! Illiterate! Get the dictionary out and read it. Metastasize means spreading, moving. You imbecile!"

She died on a rainy night in June.

Six months later, I am sitting at an old strong green Hermes typewriter in my house in Forest Hills, in Queens, writing my novel. I am squeezed between two stacks of wood. This had been our garage and a carpenter named Walter had been converting it into an office for me. He went out for lunch one day, went down the hill to Jamaica Avenue and went into the Richmond Hill Savings Bank and presented the young woman teller with a paper bag and a note saying that he would shoot her between the eyes with the gun under his jacket — he had no gun — if she did not fill the bag with all the money in the world. She filled the bag and gave it back to him. Clutching it to his bosom, he ran with his riches. Of course the teller let out some squall. It wasn't her money but she still took it personal. She came out of that bank after him. Running on the sidewalk under the El went Walter, running, running, running on the sidewalk under the El and he happened to glance down at the paper bag and saw that it was completely filled with one-dollar bills. He suffered a gallbladder attack on the spot and stopped dead. He was a statue holding a bag of single dollars when the woman teller and a simple patrolman fell on him.

He did a year and when he returned to my office to finish the job, I was still on the novel. "I built the chapel in Danbury," he said. "When you go there, you ought to look at it."

Now, deep in a late fall day, I took one page out of the typewriter and was about to put in another when exactly out of nowhere, I thought, "Ronnie Eldridge."

I had not seen her in over ten years. Her husband, Larry Eldridge, had died eleven years before this.

The first time I ever had seen her was one day in 1965 when I had to meet Bobby Kennedy at the bar of the Carlyle hotel on 76th Street. I was going to Vietnam and I wanted to hear what he had to say about it. He came in and said that he had to make a couple of stops, and would I like to come along and we could talk in the car. In the car outside was a politician, Ronnie Eldridge, the West Side Reform district leader. He always said, "Behind that sweet motherly face is one of the toughest political minds in the city, if not the country." Someday he was going to run for president and she was going to be one of the people he leaned on for extraordinary toughness.

Now in the car we spoke about Vietnam. The memory here is clear and it is startling because he said that he had been at Dien Bien Phu with his brother Jack, and they saw the French, who were trying the Vietnamese at fighting. "We thought the French were wonderful troops and that they would lose," he said.

"What are we there for?" I asked him.

He said that I should get the writings of Lin Piao, the Chinese theoretician, who in eleven pages had issued the domino theory. The paper said they would conquer one country, and each time, some of the others would collapse. Kennedy believed it and so did everybody he knew, all these geniuses who helped get kids from Ozone Park killed.

I don't remember where I got out of the car or what I said to Ronnie Eldridge, but I know I was there and she was there and

Kennedy was so wrong, as was practically everybody else in the country. Now on this afternoon all these years later, I thought of her name, nothing more, and went back to work.

Two days later, again out of nowhere, Ronnie Eldridge called me. She also must have been changing the page in her typewriter. I had not heard her voice since I called her house after her husband died. That was twelve years ago. He was forty-two and that was some shock in so many houses. The first you know of to die. This time, she said her friend Bob Gangi was trying to raise support to oppose a prison bond issue and would it interest me to write a column? What is the difference what it was about? You can fall in love sight unseen.

I made a date to have a drink with her. The usual carnage at home forced me to call and break it. And the next two dates after that.

I had an oven door hanging open. One day, one of the kids, Kelly, went to the store and brought home a cartful of food. Seven cereals, I think. She left them on the kitchen floor and disappeared. She was the last to shop.

I began to imagine, accurately and effectively, what it was like for a woman to be

128

home. Particularly at 5:30 P.M., with the day gone and the kitchen oppressive, and the noise from kids and the phone ringing wearing you down. I am the housewife, I tell myself, and the next call is going to be from the man of the house. He is going to say, "Gee, I have to meet these people for drinks, but I'll try and get out of having dinner with them. I don't know. I'll let you know."

My answer would be very simple. "You have forty-five minutes to be here or I am going out drinking myself."

Daughter Kelly was in the High School for Performing Arts. That was a famous school and the moment the mother died she simply stopped going. Her bedroom floor was covered with clothes, which she either dropped after wearing or threw on the floor as she took them out of the bureau and decided she didn't want them. I was silly enough to ask for her report card and she said that it had not arrived yet. It now was deep in July. One morning I looked in disgust at her room, kicked a warm-up jacket out of the way and here was one report card. Showing a thousand absences. I had uncontrollable fury. Once, I could show my fury against the backdrop of the mother's presence and superior authority, and, of course, they liked her better. But now I was alone and rather than an authority I became an opponent. Kelly looked me right in the eye and told me that it was not a report card at all and if I would stop sneaking into her room I would know that.

Each morning when I got up at 5:30 to make coffee, there was a glass in the sink, the best stemware, and with a little milk left in the bottom. That was my son Christopher. Not just one morning. Every morning. Sometimes there would be soda in the bottom of the glass, with the empty can of soda on the sideboard. Through fall and into midwinter, with the wind shrieking outside and sleet hitting the windows, here was the glass with milk in the bottom to start the day. In the summer, with the first pink light of day, here is soda in the bottom of the glass and the can on the sideboard.

One morning I looked at the glass and said, "Who is supposed to take care of the glass?"

And I said to myself, "You."

It was over nothing, really. A glass and a little milk. And it could over a succession of mornings drive you insane.

My six kids were split right down the middle. My older boys, twins, and the oldest daughter, Rosemary, tried to soothe me and at the same time go on with their lives. But the three youngest who were at home were having great trouble and I was not handling it by doing anything but shouting. I knew one thing: The father should go first for the kids' sake.

Then on a New Year's Eve morning I just called up Ronnie Eldridge and said, "You want a cup of coffee?" She said all right. I told her I would meet her at the Laurent Restaurant on East 56th Street, the best bar in the city, and there was not one that I didn't know. My friend John Neckland from the Woodside neighborhood was the bartender. I came into the place at 4:00 P.M. and it was absolutely empty and beautifully dim. I had Scotch and looked up and Ronnie Eldridge came to the top of the three carpeted steps leading into the bar with her lips slightly parted, smiling beautifully, and she tripped down the steps with her fur coat open, and she hurried through the tables toward me and I was in love with her right there.

Whether I realized it or not did not matter because I soon would.

She clutched her middle.

"Oh. I'm getting fat."

We had nine children between us, my six and her three, and every one of them called

131

us that afternoon at the bar at least once.

Even before we met each other that day, each of the kids knew, without being told or even having seen us, that the two of us meeting was a serious thing, and probably not recallable even by the worst tantrum. It was the tide coming up and thus unstoppable.

One morning a couple of months later, I was on the phone with her and I was saying how miserable it was living alone in Queens, which I meant, and she said, "Want to get married?"

I stammered something about yes.

"I'd love being a Rockaway housewife," she said.

The marriage part was true. Her geography was an honest mistake. She thought all of Queens meant Rockaway because that's where Irish come from. But the housewife thing was a bold-faced lie.

I am married to Ronnie M. Eldridge for thirteen years. I think that one reason you get married after a wife's death is that you simply can never again live alone. If the marriage was a bit of a bore, or no good at all, the man is in no hurry to get married, if he ever does.

I should not be able to speak for women, but in this case I sure can and fairly accurately because the word *marriage* produces one of the few emotions that they cannot successfully conceal. Women of any age want to get married, even though they know that the emotions will run their course and they will be living with some guy they tolerate but essentially don't love and barely like.

Still, they want to be married. Loneliness is a hideous problem virtually owned by women. In my time in my city there are no circumstances more desolate than those of older women who are alone. The men who divorce them go off with younger women, the closer to a child the more fervent the man's pursuit.

Then the man goes to work, this poor imbecile who is so proud of his young woman at home.

Everything I have observed shrieks that the man at work does not own the youth of the woman at home. I give you the testimony of the cop looking out the patrol car window.

Q. What is the number one thing in your day?

A. Girls! Everywhere you look, you can fall in love.

Since men die first, the widows are left in a world with few available men of their age, and, as noted, those that are around are lunging at recent high school graduates.

The only newspaper that attracts many death notices is the *New York Times* newspaper, and they are scoured each morning by women of a certain age, who are electrified by any death notice for a woman. For if she has died, then somewhere a man lives. Quickly, the eye goes over the death notice to see that a husband survives. After that, it is up to the age of the woman. In her fifties, she doesn't want to see the word *grandchildren* in the notice. "I wish they would run the age of the man," one woman I know said. For older women, if there are grandchildren mentioned, the fewer the better, forget anything past that. A great-grandchild is a synonym for nursing home.

But if the age at a glance seems acceptable, the next thing the reader does is start searching for somebody who knows the poor widower who needs comfort.

The chances are that the poor man is taken long before the wife dies because being a man and therefore very close to a rat, he seeks comforting what with the wife dying and all. Women reading the death notice have false hope because as they are reading the death notice, the widower is already out buying his girl friend Cliffs Notes because she wants to graduate from college before they get married.

Ronnie Eldridge and I don't know any other middle-aged woman and man finding each other and getting married.

For this marriage, Ronnie went around to the Stephen Wise Synagogue and asked for the female rabbi, Helene Ferris, to marry her but it could not be done. The most liberal Jewish synagogue in the nation would not condone marrying this hideous Irish Catholic.

Ronnie Eldridge's people said to her with great smugness, "That's all right. Wait'll you hear what his side has to say."

What the Catholics at St. Patrick's Cathedral had to say was whether she wanted to be married at the main altar or in the beautiful Our Lady's Chapel behind the main altar. They were so happy to have a Catholic, even a known dissenter, Breslin, reaffirm his faith that whatever we wanted we had.

Rather than such a glittering place as St. Patrick's, we were married on September 12, 1982, at Blessed Sacrament Roman Catholic Church on West 71st Street in Manhattan. We had planned the wedding for exactly three days and had two hundred friends and relatives, even though everybody in Queens thought that it would not take place. How can you go that far, all the way from the beloved Queens Boulevard to the West Side of Manhattan, just to get married? All nine kids were standing at the altar under this immense crucifix hanging from the ceiling that caused all the bride's people to be apprehensive to the point of distraction from the ceremony. But the priest, the great Monsignor Jack Barry, Uncle Jack or "UJ" as his nephews called him, asked for applause at the end of the ceremony. We walked around to her apartment on Central Park West and a rabbi came in and performed the ceremony a second time, this one in her religion, although the rabbi was in there surreptitiously, being that he wasn't supposed to be marrying one of his flock to a Catholic. I frequently recalled this with fondness and pride, even with some glee, until much later, when the absolutely unstoppable flood of scripture readings about Jews killing Christ ended my smug and superior attitude.

So we put together two families, Irish-Italian from Queens and German Jewish from the West Side of Manhattan. At the moment we were married, we had the nine children, and my wife had a mother who was in her eighties and had years and years ahead of her. From the start, she called me "him." Everybody else hated each other. My kids brought a huge bag filled with condolence letters and mass cards for my poor late wife. The letters were unopened. One of them was from Ronnie Eldridge saying, "I hope I can be as nice to you as you were to me when Larry died."

As she read it, I was dozing in bed next to her.

She put everything into a box in the basement with the notes and cards for her husband's death. "Our family history," she said.

I told you that when she proposed to me on the phone she said she wanted to be a Rockaway housewife. Absolutely marvelous. What happened was we got married, we stayed where she lived on West 67th Street in Manhattan. I found that in her whole life she had not moved more than twenty blocks from where she was born and raised. Which takes care of the word *Rockaway*. The housewife part of it was a bold-faced lie from the go. About the first thing she did as a bride, she ran in an eight-way Democratic primary for the city council seat on the West Side of Manhattan. "I'll only do it this one time," she said. "If I win, I'll serve one term and that will do it."

At seven o'clock one morning a woman

carrying a clipboard walked right into the bedroom. I had never seen her before. She was furious that I was in bed.

"Where is Ronnie? We must do the subway stop at 72nd Street."

"And you are?"

"Eva Lederman from the campaign. I was Bella Abzug's high school gym teacher. I was a lieutenant in the navy during the war, you know. I was a registered Communist. G-2 really screwed up with me, didn't they? Is your wife in the shower? Tell her to hurry up. We're late already."

That went on for six weeks, and through every day my wife kept saying, "Just this one time. You can live through it. I'm not going to do it again." And the dining room table was taken up by people going over election lists.

She won the eight-way primary wonderfully well. That night, there was a large crowd of her people in Jack Donahue's on West 72nd Street. She made a speech and they all clapped. I got tired and went home. Nobody knew I was gone.

At 6:30 the following morning, she swings out of bed and hits the floor with a thump.

"What are you doing up?" I said.

"Labor breakfast."

"What are you going there for? You won

the thing last night, remember?"

"Don't be silly. This is how you get reelected."

I was remembering this as I stood out on this terrace now, in the cold and with the plants dead for the season. I decided that as long as I'm thinking of dying, I might as well wonder what would happen when I'm dead and she is dead, too, and we all were together someplace. There would be the first to go, Rosemary Breslin and Larry Eldridge, and then Jimmy Breslin and Ronnie Eldridge.

To whom would we turn?

Would both the others demand the original? And would both of us want that, too?

Or would we stay as we are?

And what about the first two? Would they be waiting for us?

Or is love and friendship from the earth so tiny when placed against an eternity that it is not even noticeable in Heaven? Or could there be so much love in the very atmosphere of Heaven, coming upon each breath and through every pore?

Once, in one of these observations to cause me discomfort, Ronnie said that I undoubtedly would go with Rosemary because we were Catholics and had a place to go and she being Jewish and not believing in God, or His heaven and hell, would be on the outside of whatever this place was and for all of eternity.

"I think there is someplace where Larry is, circling around, like a bird, I guess. I can almost feel it sometimes. But I can't envision much more."

I insisted that this was nonsense, that the hereafter belongs to the good and that means all of us.

We stopped right there because accepting this meant that you next had to consider the limitless future of the already dead and the real possibility that we might even be called upon to choose, which I could not believe but could not disprove, either.

Besides, the number one thing in the life lived by all is, do not disturb the illusion.

3

When I was first starting to cover stories, I went to the auction of the great horse Nashua, in the main offices of the Hanover Bank, then at 60 Broadway. Nashua's owner, William Woodward Jr., had been shot by his wife, who said she mistook him for a prowler in their Long Island home. The racing stable was put up for auction. Nashua was separate. Nashua was a great champion. They took the returns at the bank. I entered this large room that was an entire floor of this old financial district building. It looked like a retired general had designed the interior. The desks were spaced precisely from windows to wall. The men sitting at them were young and looked like gray wood. I showed up in my best reporter's clothes, raincoat for winter wear — we were in December — no tie, button missing from the jacket, pockets stuffed with notebooks and paper. I was at once misplaced and yet in command of myself and everything around me; I said I wanted coffee and a flunky ran it to me. I looked over the big room and my eyes met one fellow of about my age. He had short light hair and the beginning of jowls. He wore a gray suit with a vest and a pocket watch, with the chain draped across his front. Somebody's son, I told myself. Living in the past and he isn't even forty. I looked at him and he looked at me and he thought he saw excitement and I knew I saw a prisoner. Although if I had that watch of his, I would have had it pawned by three o'clock. A crowd of reporters stood around a thin man with big round glasses whose hands were nervous because of all the reporters watching him open envelopes. He said the winning bid was a million two hundred fifty thousand, two hundred dollars. At that time, in 1955, Nashua was at Aqueduct Race Track, in a stall about five hundred yards off Rockaway Boulevard. I lived three short blocks away. I never heard of anything in Ozone Park that was worth a million dollars. I remember walking out of the big bank room and the guy sitting at the desk following me with his eyes as I walked out in the freedom I found in my business.

Afterward, I saw Nashua brought out to a field at Spendthrift Farm in Lexington, Kentucky. Since the horse had been able to stand up he had been led, held, urged, struck, kicked and tied into a stall like he had been caught stealing. Now Nashua had just been taken out of racing for a few months and he was being brought into this great field of waving limestone-fed Kentucky bluegrass and now the groom reached up and began to take off his halter. I saw the horse photographer, J. C. Skeets Meadors, shiver with excitement. He had the camera up and ready when they let Nashua go for the first time in the life he could remember.

And the horse swooped, his head low, almost skimming the grass and now pounding, pounding, pounding, dirt flying in the air, snorting, whinnying, he ran in every direction. He ran that way for most of the day. Lord, did that horse teach me a lesson in freedom, and I think it always showed in whatever I did and how I lived while I did it.

Now look at me. Here I am carrying the poster of a patient, a big brown envelope containing my angiogram film and I am on my way to show it to another doctor. My daily life has been given up to doctors, nurses, doctor's receptionists, datebooks. We know I have an aneurysm and there seems no question that I will wind up in Phoenix, Arizona. Still all the young people in the family with their printouts have me running around like an old bellman, surly and reluctant, while they keep slamming the counter bell to summon me and tell me to read this, go there.

Coming out of the subway at 168th Street in Washington Heights, on my way to Columbia Presbyterian Hospital across the street, I glanced up at the scarred, green facade of the old Audubon Ballroom. Once, I had gone to a fight there, Jimmy Herring of Linden Boulevard, Ozone Park, boxing at middleweight, starting a comeback by defeating Ralph (Tiger) Jones. I sat in the last row and drank beer.

Then one cold Sunday morning in January of 1965, I went to this old scarred barren hall to see Malcolm X, who also was trying a comeback in the Audubon. By now, his was only a thin following, but he was working on a Sunday, and I needed a column for the Monday paper.

On this slow news Sunday, I went upstairs to the main floor of the Audubon and into the back, where the fighters used to get dressed, and I was smoking a Pall Mall cigarette there. You couldn't smoke at a Muslim gathering.

But you could shoot guns. There was shouting in the Audubon that Sunday. Malcolm X had his hands held out and some

144

guy running up the aisle, in a short black leather jacket, blew him down with a sawed-off shotgun. The noise shook the old building. By the time I looked out, Malcolm had been shot down. Afterward they pushed Malcolm X on a gurney across Broadway to the hospital. The crowd around the gurney shook their fists and howled for revenge.

In the Audubon, a uniformed cop asked if anybody had any chalk.

People shrugged. The cop went down to the street and across to a candy store. He came back with a long piece of fresh white chalk. He drew a chalk outline of Malcolm X's body as it had been sprawled on the stage. He did it very well, drawing freehand, and had one of Malcolm's arms bent, just as it had been before they carried him off.

For so many years I never went to a murder or accident scene where they did not have a chalk outline of the victim on the highway, sidewalk, staircase or floor —

— On the floor of a barroom in Maspeth, in Queens, where three young Hispanics came in and shot an off-duty cop dead. The cop lived around the corner with his Puerto Rican wife, who came running down the street screaming. She was afraid to touch the chalk line drawn around her husband's body.

— On 63rd Street in Manhattan a construction worker stepped on a board jutting out from the twentieth floor and the board tipped. His hands grabbed at the air and he was gone without a sound. A cop went to the Catholic school off Lexington Avenue and came back with a piece of yellow chalk and drew the outline around the construction worker's body, a precise yellow chalk outline that made you appreciate what a good job the cop had done freehand at the Malcolm X crime scene.

Then I started to notice that older cops or rescue workers stepped nonchalantly on the chalk, obliterating parts of the outline, as if the chalk had no meaning.

It did not. It was as useful as paper blowing down the street. Somebody had used chalk once somewhere, then another did the same thing and without a thought of what it was about, it became a rite of tragedy.

I came to understand that the chalk lines represented death surprising everybody, leaving families so defenseless and dejected, alone without notice. And as the outline is drawn on the sidewalk in the harsh light of emergency lamps, it speaks for the worth of a life: the money you made, the business titles you held, the house you owned, the clothes you wore, the cars you drove.

All as meaningless as chalk.

Here are the morgue workers taking away the body. Left is this record of life in chalk that gets rubbed out, starting with the first foot to come along, or suddenly washed completely away by a thick white rain lashing the sidewalk.

I never noticed the chalk outline of my body that was only a few feet away from me every day for so long. I was pulled back from it by a miracle I could not see. I was only a step away for so long. I haven't a single solitary idea of why I received such fortune. Deserving nothing, I get all.

Without such a break, what tale would the chalk have told about me? That I had six children and walked them to school sometimes and took them on trips? That I married a second time and my wife had three children and that gave us nine and you can trust them all? That I worked for decades in newspapers, and tried to tell the truth and still beat the newspaper business to a pulp, so much so that they hired five people with Irish names to try to imitate me? It's terrific, and it could be far better if they all sent me a commission every week and then I wouldn't have to go to work. That I lived in a fine house in Queens and two spectacular apartments in Manhattan?

That now I wear good suits made by a tailor but because I step into so many puddles while out working, and wind up tramping on the wet cuffs, that the suit cuffs are always frayed? That I have a Pulitzer Prize to show for my years but now I can't even get a last look at it because it is in with the chalk?

The real worth of any life is in all those things that the chalk does not show. What you failed to do destroys you. The Sins of Omission. One turned back can wipe out a lifetime.

Still, the temptation is to stand up on your last day for pleading and say:

I give you thanks, O Lord, that I am not like the rest of them here today. These grasping, crooked, adulterous people. I try to be very good. I contribute to your church. I try to keep holy the Sabbath. I don't kill. If you had given me a little notice, even a few hours in a bed, where I could collect a few thoughts and then drift off, I would have had a better presentation. But as you know this thing came on so fast that I truly didn't even know it. So, I guess all I can do now is point out that I'm a lot better than what's around here today.

If you believe in orderly planning of a life, best leave the house each day with a piece of chalk in your pocket. In mythology that becomes true, Aeschylus was threatened with the fall of a house and took every precaution and then got himself killed by a form of roof — the shell of a tortoise dropped by a flying eagle.

I crossed the street from the building where they killed Malcolm X and walked to the neurological building, which was down a gloomy side street, one side of which was the high sand-colored hospital complex. That ended at the West Side Highway and across the highway and down a grassy bank was the Hudson River with New Jersey rising from its shores. On the other side of the street from the hospital was an old armory that was filled with the homeless and drug and alcohol addicts. Around all this was the neighborhood of Washington Heights, four- and five-story attached buildings packed with people from the Dominican Republic. There are 500,000 of them living in this small area with everything in the modern world wrong; most need jobs and live on streets filled with bicycles and baby strollers and cars triple-parked, many with New Jersey license plates, the suburban white drivers buying drugs as Dominican mothers walk by with their children in strollers. The police precinct for the area, the 30th, had officers who would steal manhole covers.

And then the Dominicans have everything that is magical and thrilling about all the years of immigrants in New York. They are a handsome people, fast and bright, and so politically active that people running for office in the Dominican Republic come to Washington Heights for a month at a time, asking for support. Soon, this love of politics, the voices roaring through megaphones, the music and the colorful banners, will be evident in any election of any size in New York. There is no city on earth with so much in front of it. And as you walk this block to the hospital entrance, you only have to remind yourself that there is another colony like this, of 500,000 Haitians in Flatbush in Brooklyn. There they speak French.

It gives me an empty feeling every time I think of going to Phoenix. And immediately I hope that one of these New York hospitals the children send me to will fit.

This was Thursday, November 17.

Late Thursday afternoon in Phoenix, Gianni Vishteh, third-year resident in neurosurgery, Barrow Neurological Institute, remembers, the residents and medical students sat on office chairs or stood behind the chairs and watched all these lives appear as a tangle of blood vessels on a lighted board on the wall. There were about twenty-five residents, all young, all leaning forward, eager to see. They were in operating room green or blue shirts and pants. They came from the operating rooms down the hall and into this radiology room of the Barrow Neurological Institute.

The head of neurosurgery, Robert Spetzler, in a green operating room cap, sits sideways in the front, his elbow at the board, looking at the audience. He is conducting what is called "rounds." This sounds like they walk through the rooms and look at the patients, but in this case "rounds" means that they sit and look at angiogram film that has been sent in by other doctors from all over on behalf of patients who need surgery. Sitting opposite Spetzler is the third-year resident, Vishteh. He presses a button and with a grinding sound the rows of pictures, a dozen across, four and five rows of them for a case, move up. They look, comment, question, decide, the alternator grinds and the pictures go up and another set appears.

With each set, Vishteh reads from a diagnosis. Then he comes to the angiogram film brought by David Chalif, a neurosurgeon from North Shore Hospital and New

York University. I had met him at NYU and at the end of a clear, tremendously impressive recitation of my situation and what had to be done, he mentioned Spetzler. I said that maybe I would go down to Phoenix and Chalif said that he would be there next week himself. He wanted to watch some methods that Spetzler used. Which told me all I needed to know. With my pictures on the lighted wall, Chalif does the voice-over, which, in record and recollection by participant Vishteh, said:

CHALIF: This is a sixty-five-year-old male presented to me complaining of a left eye condition that is closed. The pupil is normal. He denies any significant headaches, denies any progression of symptoms. History of two to three years of Diabetes, diet and Glynase controlled. Left third nerve palsy beginning in October with subsequent extensive workup revealing a lacuna and aneurysm of the right cerebral artery with unruptured 6 mm anterior communicating artery aneurysm, pointing down. A 0.5 cm density at the junction of the right anterior cerebral artery and the anterior communicating artery . . .

SPETZLER: Stop.

SPETZLER: (to a resident) What do you do?

RESIDENT: Hmmmm.

SPETZLER: Hup, hup, I don't have all day.

RESIDENT: Abnormality in the anterior communicating complex.

SPETZLER: Meaning what?

RESIDENT: Anterior communicating artery aneurysm (pointing to the head of the aneurysm on angiogram).

SPETZLER: What do you want to do?

RESIDENT: Refer it to Sonntag. [He is another surgeon, known for work on spines.]

SPETZLER: You better start packing your bags. Tonight.

Vishteh says it was said with apparent humor.

As with all the other cases, no name was given. I was a sixty-five-year-old male. Apparently that is the proper form and later I was to appreciate this lack of personality being involved very much.

SPETZLER: This is a classic anterior communicating artery aneurysm. However, it could be more complex than it is supposed to be. It is situated in the area where there is the danger of the most devastation on intellectual faculties. The approach must be in the front, right above the eyes cavity.

(To Chalif) We'll be happy to take the case.

The file is given to Vishteh, an Iranian who has relatives in the upper Bronx. He is a lanky twenty-nine-year-old who says that Barrow residents are what his favorite team, the old Oakland Raiders, once claimed to be. Aggressive and conform to nobody. His own education consists of the University of Pittsburgh medical school, which is at least extraordinarily prestigious, and a rating in the top five percent of medical students in the country. So the old Raiders are all in his mind.

I was home when Vishteh called from Spetzler's office. He said the angiogram film looked like I was a good candidate for an aneurysm operation. I remember his voice was low. Since the subject was slightly important to me, I immediately dropped into an unexcited, plodding comprehension of what he was telling me.

"When do I come?" I asked him.

"You'll have to speak to the secretary," he said.

He put me through to a secretary.

She came on. "When would you like to come?"

"Anytime starting Monday," I said.

"We'll see you here at two on Monday."

"When do you think I'd have the operation?"

"On Tuesday morning at 8:30."

"How long will I be in the hospital, do you think?"

She said she didn't know.

"I have to work," I said. I said it without any sense of sounding deranged. Years of needing money caused me to look around mistrustfully at any absence from work, even for a life in danger.

4

Right now, I have to question myself closely. If I am trying to come up with some kind of a Last Memory, don't even bother because the only thing I can think of just now out of my whole life is being broke.

Have you ever been broke in your life? It's a nice feeling, isn't it? How do I feel this morning? Great. I don't have to go anywhere. You know why I don't have to go anywhere? Because I don't have the carfare to get off the corner.

The first newspaper building where I ever worked, the *Long Island Press* newspaper, was at what used to be the last stop of the El, in Jamaica, in the center of south Queens, in the hollow of the great city. Queens is flat and dull and then abruptly ends at wet sands of an ocean. Now the three-story Press building in Jamaica is empty, the bricks dead. Today, they would flock to it from every shelter and sidewalk grating because of a beggar's delight, an unattended door that went from the street right onto the staircase to the city room. Through this door, in a tweed overcoat so coated with grease that you could cook pancakes on it, came Joe Gould, the famous poet and bum from Greenwich Village. He didn't come for any research. He arrived to panhandle. A dollar would do, he said. After all, he had been on the subway all the way out here to the last stop. He deserved something, he said. Gottlieb, the editor, had to come up with two dollars. Then Gould tried the rest of the city room. Si Newhouse, the owner's son, sat by the window and ate Nedick's hot dogs for lunch and wrote police stories and hunched over like a man under guerrilla attack when Gould appeared. I told Gould, fuck you, old man. He talked about his roommate, Max Bodenheim. I didn't know who Bodenheim was, but I figured that he got half the take, being that he was Gould's roommate. So the two of them could go and fuck themselves.

The first day that my friend Fred Mc-Morrow came to work on the newspaper, I said to him, "You want lunch?"

"I think I'll wait awhile," he said.

"I'm going out now," I said.

"When I get paid on Friday I'll have lunch," he said.

That wasn't trying to make me smile. He

would have lunch when he got paid and that was five days away. And don't look at me in the meantime. After work, McMorrow said he was going for dinner. We walked under the El to the Bickford's Cafeteria. They had Jell-O with whipped cream in the window. Inside in the gloom McMorrow said to the woman at the counter, "Could I have bread, please? I forgot to get it with the order." She handed him bread and he went to the table and grabbed the catsup bottle and poured it on the bread, which he folded in half and that was it. Folded one piece in half for a sandwich. I grabbed the other.

That is all that newspaper life was to me and the people I came up with. Having no money was the whole game.

It was also a danger to the public, too. Newspaper owners trying to keep all the money had staffs that didn't get paid enough to keep them remotely honest. The sports editor of the *Press* newspaper used to get ten dollars a week from Madison Square Garden. The papers also had too few reporters working to protect the public by trying to discover the truth of the times. One Sunday, I was detached from baseball box scores at the *Press* and went to LaGuardia Field, whose arrivals and departures were still regarded as news. There were a thousand photos of pretty girls waving from the top of the staircase. The wing and engines blocked any chance of seeing up their dresses. The readers wanted sex and they were getting an advertisement for engine thrust.

At about 1:30 that afternoon at LaGuardia, I followed Tom Poster, who was covering the airport for the AP, up to a National Airlines plane where, standing on the stairs in the flashbulbs, was Senator Joseph McCarthy. He was a moon-faced drunk from Wisconsin who was a homophobe, for the usual reasons apparently, and he made American history by holding a hunt for Communists that went on only because of the cowardice of all but a couple of politicians, and almost all newspapers from front page to editorials. He said the State Department was made of Communists and homosexuals and they were responsible for the whole of China turning Communist. One billion people turn Communist while two bureaucrats consort in a YMCA in Washington. He said movie and television writers and actors were in a cabal to hand America over to Russia. Eisenhower, winner of a whole world war, was afraid to oppose the man. There were hearts broken, hopes crushed, decency dropped on the sidewalk.

McCarthy is old history, of the 1950s, but you can be fifteen today and with an IQ of 75 and still understand that if you don't know about him, it could cause pain today, tomorrow and maybe forever in your life. For there can be no way that another big dumb driven half a fascist will not come through some congressional chamber bawling for control and censorship of all these cables and computer networks, and speech comes next. You never lose your freedom all at once; the books show it happens one slice at a time. And don't count on the people in crowds. At the airport on this day, it was amazing how many people who were going to other planes began calling out, "God bless you, Senator McCarthy." I had not paid much attention to McCarthy before this. What did I know? Except for this one day, I was in a sports department pasting up box scores and "Fights Last Night." With a wide smile, McCarthy said, "Hello, Tom," to Poster. He knew Poster from all the times he had flown in. He took one look at me and saw that I looked Irish and figured that made me all right.

"What brings you to town, Senator?" Poster asked.

"Well, Tom, I'm on my way to Washington. I couldn't make mass in Appleton this morning or I'd have missed the plane. Well, when the plane was starting to come in here, I looked at my watch and saw that I just had time to make a last mass. I can get another plane from here to Washington later on."

Poster remembers that as McCarthy talked, he was looking over the fringes of the crowd at someone who seemed to be waiting for him. One of the arts of being a Catholic at that time was to know the times of every mass in the city. Poster and I knew that the last mass in the whole city already had gone off at 1:05 P.M. and that was in Manhattan, by Penn Station. Here was McCarthy, at 1:45 in the afternoon at LaGuardia, saying he was going to mass. McCarthy wasn't making a mistake, because nobody makes that big a mistake. He might as well have had the day of the week wrong.

I was there to pick up a photo holder. I took it back to the office, and also typed a note about McCarthy lying about mass, but it was too far out of the ordinary.

After work, I went to Glenn's Bar in Richmond Hill and I had some good big cold beer and announced, "I don't know what they do in Washington, but I can tell you that the guy is an effin' liar in Queens. If he lies about mass, how can you believe him about anything?"

It was a serious charge, which in the morning was remembered by everyone as slander of a saint.

All these years later and I am standing in Gargiulio's Restaurant in Coney Island, in Brooklyn, which is a movie set for the day, a movie of a book I wrote, *The Gang That Couldn't Shoot Straight*. Ready for a scene is a new actor, Robert De Niro, in his first major movie at $750 a week, and suddenly through the door with this electrifying walk comes the great Lionel Stander. Ask people right now who he was and they tell you that he was Robert Wagner's butler on the television series *Hart to Hart*. This was only a last act, with great pay, to the career of an impressive American. He had first been immensely popular in *Mr. Deeds Goes to Town* with Gary Cooper. Now, *The Gang* is his first American movie since McCarthy's days. They insisted that Lionel was a Communist. Called before a House Un-American Activities Committee hearing in New York, he came through the doors and up the aisle with a woman on each arm. He got them good seats and sat at a microphone and delivered a loud, rousing, brilliant, endless monologue about the Ku Klux Klan and American fascists. He was great. The next day on the golf course in Los Angeles, Harry Cohn of Columbia Pictures told Stander's agent, "Tell him he's through. So are you if you have any more to do with him." The agent immediately called Stander. "Don't even come back here to collect your clothes." Lionel had to go to Rome to get any work. I sit with him for a few minutes over coffee and I tell Lionel about the McCarthy business and that it was a shame I couldn't have written something decent.

"And it is a terrible tragedy that I was so stupid that I had to go through this to learn anything," he roars.

"What?" I asked.

"That these people must be slain before they reach kindergarten!"

So he strides to the bar and points at my friend Fat Thomas and says:

"When we have the revolution, you are going to be First Commissar!

"The liberals," he bellowed, "I will have all the liberals taken out and put against a wall and then there will be no more effin' liberals."

"Mr. Stander?" It is the director.

"Yes."

"Are you ready, sir?"

"Certainly."

And Lionel Stander strode out to the set where he played his first scene in America in a quarter of a century. He played it with an actor who had the first movie role of his life, Robert De Niro.

Stander wound up on the television series *Hart to Hart* at a living wage, maybe $20,000 a week.

But still, I know myself well enough that I would have blithely risked it all, whatever was coming, column, book, movie, the works, if I ever had a chance that day at the airport to write something about McCarthy that would have caused trouble.

The McCarthy of today must be so much stronger because the territory is vast. You can have laws against viewing or showing something and the general public, sheep to be sheared, will nod dumbly. But there are people who instantly will find a way around any rule. Enforcement would require tremendous diligence. I'll show you. I see my movies now in Loretta's apartment in the Pink Houses in East New York. She sits with her pink bathrobe pulled around her and watches any of the two thousand movies on videotape, all of them bootlegged. The last time she went to a regular movie was at the Duffield Theatre. "I took a little nap for myself and a man falls from the balcony

right into the next seat. Shot in the head."
She went home for good. Shortly thereafter,
the projectionist quit after a hundred shots
were fired in the movie house. Nobody else
had the guts to take the job, so the Duffield
closed.

Loretta sat home in her pink robe and
saw just about every movie that came out,
some of them only hours after their pre-
miere. I must have seen fifty of them. Her
first bootleg tapes were made by people in
her neighborhood, who just walked into a
movie house and set up a video camera in
the aisle and shot the feature film up on the
screen. If a security guard came down to
bother them, they either threatened to shoot
him or did shoot him, and the sad thing
about that is that it is no overstatement.
The trouble with their work was that often
the videotape was dark or you could hear
the sound of the neighborhood cameraman
eating popcorn as he taped the show. When
I saw the *Malcolm X* movie at Loretta's
house, there was the sound of a baby in the
movie house crying and fussing and the
voice of the bootleg cameraman calling out,
"Bitch, get the baby out of the movie. Get
that baby somethin' to eat."

Loretta paid five dollars for each tape
and then had neighbors in for popcorn and

soda and charged them three dollars each to see the movie. They all hated *Natural Born Killers* because they couldn't get into any of the killing. There had been five real murders around the place in the last few weeks and people walked hunched over in the living room in case of a stray shot coming through the window. But they were ecstatic over the movie *Quiz Show*. The quality was much better because Loretta used a new bootlegger. "He is a dude from India who gets us the best tapes," she said. "He wears a red turban. I call him 'Roger.' Indians, they thieves like anybody else." She introduced *Quiz Show* by saying, "This one show how the whites started stealin'."

5

The thing I have, an aneurysm, wasn't discovered until these German pathologists in the 1880s found them in autopsies. I learn this by getting into the New York University Medical School Library, on the ground floor of the building on First Avenue. It's good. You can read about what's wrong, and then go next door to the city morgue and take a firsthand look. I went through one book on neurosurgery that was so heavy that the woman at the desk should have given me a hand truck. Then I became fanatically interested in the pages because of an account of the first brain surgeons.

They didn't even have brain surgery worth keeping records on until Harvey Cushing came around at Harvard in 1910 or so. Harvey Cushing practically invented neurosurgery and he used to go in there with neither light nor anesthesia. Cushing had a daughter, Betsy, who married John Hay Whitney of New York. I know the woman. Now this is a meaningless thing thrown in, except that Whitney is the man who helped me go from busted valise to half a big shot and that makes my statement, that Cushing's daughter married him, more important news to me than a building collapse.

Cushing wrote at night and won a Pulitzer Prize for biography. His genius was not too burdened with sentiment. A doctor named Dandy did the first aneurysm operations. Cushing helped him tremendously. He was such a stand-up guy that when he heard how good Dandy was he offered him a big job at Harvard. Dandy sells his house in Baltimore, quits his post at Johns Hopkins and comes up to Harvard. Cushing looks up and says that he forgot to tell Dandy, but there is no job. That is one way to kill opposition, but Dandy was too good. He went back to Johns Hopkins and continued to work in the very beginnings of brain surgery. He cut into you with a coal miner's headlamp strapped to his head. It gave weak light for trying to find the way around the inside of somebody's head. The brain's identifying marks are hard to find at best. At that time the surgeon got inside and unconsciously waited for somebody somehow to give him another light and then he realized that this was all there was, that he was alone in pale light. How did he do? He did terrible, that's how he did. But just like Moniz, who started that angiogram thing I had earlier, he kept forging ahead, never looking down at the now-former patients as they were carted off. Actually, this is very poor phrasing on my part. The medical people like to say, "We did not obtain a good result." That means the patient did not make it.

Dandy had no powerful microscopes to help him see. Once he located the aneurysm, he had no modern magic clip to use. Dandy tied the aneurysm with a suture. How did that go? He did not obtain such great results. Later on, while the recovered person was walking around, sometimes the thread in his head parted as if hit by a big lake bass.

But as Dandy was first, a couple of brilliant tries that were frustrated yesterday might help me today.

Suddenly I am at the center of science, which at the end of millions of experiments, after centuries of learning and teaching of medicine, does not have the slightest conception of what I am.

And if I'm the only one who can die or live a damaged life here, then I am going to do the defining.

I am consciousness, and science cannot

define what that is. Religion does. I am alive and have free will but there are consequences to everything because judgment arrives with death.

Q. Who made me?

A. God made me.

This is what I learned forever when young, starting before I knew, when I slept in a baby carriage outside the church during Sunday mass. I have believed it ever since and now at this moment hold on to it with all my subconscious, with all my memory, with all that I have been taught and told.

The word *brain* always represented a fearful mystery to me. My brain can stop remembering and I won't even know the way home.

There is no way to foresee or prevent this. The brain is not just an organ. Nor is there any synonym for it. It is incomparable. It cannot be compared to anything on earth because it does nothing else but think. It weighs three pounds. It has no nickname. Your hand is a paw, the heart a ticker. The brain is the brain. If I had to make a bet I would say that the mind is a ghost from God that comes from the sky and lives in the brain. But it still uses the brain as its home, and therefore I like my brain quite a bit. Mine has given me whatever of life I have seen. If there is such a thing as owing something to your brain, then I am first on line.

Mike Tyson gets up and says, "I am thankful for being allowed to have the strength in my fists to mash my opponent's head like a turnip and maybe kill him right in the ring on Monday night."

Or Miss Mississippi stands out there on the stage at the Miss America contest and tells the judges, "Well, I'm just so thankful for my cute little fanny. I just *know* I drive men *in*-sane."

I want to thank my brain for what it has done for me. I like my brain. It is the last brain I'm going to get. It didn't make me a concert pianist or an international physicist, but I never deserved that. The brain knows exactly what you should get. I work for newspapers, write a few books, and that's exactly what I should do, that's that for you, Breslin. Oh, my brain can get good and confused. But then in a matter of utmost importance to me, it has delivered with the speed of a spark. I grew up being afraid of my feelings and suddenly my brain finds a way to make them my main strength. I replaced my feelings with what I felt were the feelings of others, and that changed with each thing I went to, so I was about sixty-seven different people in my life. Once, I sat on the edge of my bed and watched six saloon bums who are defendants in an attempted murder case listening to the verdict. Suddenly, I become the one on the end, not an evil-looking guy, a young guy praying with his entire face that he gets another chance, that they say not guilty. The jury foreman says, "Guilty." The young guy crumples. He bends over and throws up. Right away, I fall backward onto the bed. My wife calls in. "Come on for dinner." At this moment, I can't get up. I call out to her, "I can't. I just got convicted of attempted murder." She thought it was amusing. I did not. I could smell the jail cell. When I was out reporting on people, for a long time I looked for people to identify with at a distance because at first I had to keep them emotionally at arm's length and later when I got over this, I was afraid to let others even see what interested me. It caused me to work alone and I became nervous if others were around the same news.

I went to Dallas on November 22, 1963, when Kennedy was shot, and I thought that every minute of every hour I ever had worked had prepared me for writing about this. This is a marvelous emotion for you to have when a guy with a wife and two kids gets shot dead. That is called news reporting. I knew one thing: There would be several hundred reporters everywhere, but if I had any of them around me, then I was in the wrong place.

In the morning of the next day, Saturday, November 23, I walked down the highway as it sloped from the Texas School Book Depository Building. The Texas asphalt went sloping, sloping to an underpass. As you walked, that high window in the school-book building burned into your back. Your shoulders hunched. Just a few yards to the underpass. I broke into a run. Just get to the underpass. But short of the underpass here was the white chalk to show where the shots had hit Kennedy. There had been no body to be outlined, so one of the cops had drawn a large X. Look at the chalk X in the dull sun on the Texas asphalt and see the Kennedy titles and gaudiness and houses, boats and private planes. He had his own plane!

Titles are in the chalk here. Congressman, Senator, President. Leader of the Free World. Stare hard at the chalk and hear trumpets and the clamorous, building, screaming excitement and waves of shriek-ing adulation all over the world. Standing there that day in November, I wondered if he ever had a choice between this grandness that shines brilliantly, especially if recently polished to keep any traces of the temporal away, and an important life with his two children growing up around him. Of course he had a choice, and he made the wrong one. He wound up with a few instants of apparent importance. Then he got a bullet in his brain and he left two children he never knew without a father.

In Dallas, I was the only one to speak to the doctor, Malcolm Perry, who had been standing over Kennedy at the moment he died. There were three thousand reporters at the funeral in Washington, and on the packed White House driveway there was Haile Selassie of Ethiopia and Charles de Gaulle standing together, Selassie in a gaudy uniform, with his hat barely as high as the hip of de Gaulle, whose uniform looked like an old sweat suit. I became frantic. I knew I could not perform the simplest act of this very simple business of reporting if I had to do it in these crowded circumstances. I went into the White House lobby and from nowhere I thought of the cemetery. I told Art Buchwald, who wrote for my paper, "I'm going to go over to the cemetery and get the gravedigger."

Right away he liked it. "That would be very good." That is all the encouragement you ever should need; one nod from a smart guy.

The gravedigger's name was Clifton Pollard and on Sunday he was in the middle of bacon and eggs when he received the phone call he had been expecting. It was from Mazo Kawalchik, who was the foreman of gravediggers at Arlington Cemetery, which was where Polly worked for a living as a $3.01-an-hour gravedigger. "Polly, could you please be here by eleven o'clock this morning?" Mazo said. "I guess you know what it's for. Sorry to pull you out like this on a Sunday."

Polly said, "Why, it's an honor."

At the bottom of the hill in front of the Tomb of the Unknown Soldier, Pollard started digging with a reverse hoe. When the yellow teeth of the reverse hoe first bit into the ground and brought up most handsome soil, Pollard said he wanted to save it because the machine had made some tracks in the grass and he wanted to fill them in and get some good grass growing. "I'd like to have everything, you know, nice."

Another gravedigger said he would take the extra-good soil back to the garage and grow good turf on it. Pollard sat on his machine and said, "They're going to come and put him right here in this grave I'm making up. You know, it's an honor just for me to do this."

I told Pollard I'd meet him at the funeral, and I kept looking but he never showed. All day Wednesday while the world watched Kennedy being put into the ground, the man who dug the hole was on the other side of the hill, digging graves for dead servicemen for $3.01 an hour. When I finally saw him later, he said he didn't know who the new graves were for, but he expected them to be used.

"You didn't even want to see the funeral?" I asked him.

"I tried to go over," he said. "But a soldier told me it was too crowded and he couldn't let me through. I'll get over there later a little bit. Just sort of look around and see how it is, you know. Like I told you, it's an honor."

That story is used in most journalism schools. It is called the Gravedigger Theory of news coverage. Still, today, when you have a great story, you have smart editors telling reporters, "Go find the gravedigger."

It came out of my brain on a big day, when I needed something strong, and it made me look like five million dollars and

I thank my brain.

They can draw diagrams and write with great assurance that if something goes wrong on the right side of your brain, then the left side of your body will be afflicted. How do they know that? Because they have seen all those thousands and thousands of patients whose cells have died on the right side of the brain and immediately the tongue is tied and the left side of the body caves in. Nowhere has anybody seen the mind. They can see on one of the magic machines the dead brain cells that wreck a leg. But not the mind.

I am at this moment about seventy-two hours away from having my head opened. Before this, I want to listen to somebody who might know or sit with any book with the word *brain* in the title.

"Here, let me help," the clerk at the Cornell Medical School bookstore said. I had just paid him a lot for a high, heavy stack of books. I told him that I might as well get used to carrying the weight.

"Do you have a car outside?" he asked.

"No. The only thing waiting for me outside is the sidewalk."

"How many people are you delivering these to?" he asked.

"Nobody. They're all for me. I'm going

to learn them all over the weekend."

"You can't learn anything like that. You'll forget it all."

"I only have to learn these things for one time," I said.

I begin. I read that Harvard University has a skull with a hole in it that could let in a winter storm. In the same collection is a three-foot, seven-inch iron spike that was one and a quarter inches in diameter. It weighed thirteen and a half pounds. Skull and iron once belonged to a man named Phineas Gage, a blaster building the Rutland & Burlington Railroad in Vermont. His job was to drill into limestone, fill the hole with powder, put in a fuse, cover the powder with sand and then tamp the sand down with the big iron spike. After which he was to light the fuse and get out of the way. So on this day, Phineas had the hole drilled and chock full of powder and there was an interruption of some kind and Phineas neglected to pour the sand over the powder and instead he began banging the iron spike to tamp down the powder. We say he began banging because there is no record of which bang it was that caused the hole to blow up in his poor face. The rod came through Phineas Gage's chin and right straight up through the top of his head. It went through the brain searing hot and nice.

The railroad doctor called to the scene was so fascinated that, after the spike was pulled out, he put one finger through the top of Phineas' head and had another come up through the chin. "They are touching!" one account had the doctor saying proudly and excitedly.

Somehow, Gage lived. He was a little different. Where once he had been cheerful Irish with everybody around him happy and havin' a drink, now he was a dark, mean little man who caused decent people to flee when he came around. He wound up lecturing at medical schools and in freak shows at circuses. He died at thirty-eight, and Harvard Medical School got his skeleton and tamping iron.

This was in 1866. The medical exhibit I used in the hours before a brain operation was Junior Ayala's father, Naftly. I was just coming now from seeing them at the airport freight forwarding building where they work. Junior is twenty-four, and father Naftly is fifty. He had been an airlines catering manager until he fell on the back of his head two years ago and spent three weeks in a coma. When he woke up he said he was twenty-one. He has not changed.

When Naftly came home from the hospital, he said he wanted coffee and cigarettes right away. When his wife didn't bring them immediately, he pounded the table.

Junior and his mother took the father to doctors, who tried placing Naftly into Creedmoor State Hospital. The hospital said he belonged at home. He could not read. Junior put on cartoon shows. The father stared.

Maria, the wife, worked at a supermarket and Junior was at the freight forwarding company at Kennedy Airport. They needed both salaries and couldn't stay home with the father. So at 4:00 A.M. one Monday Junior shook his father awake and took him to the airport.

Junior didn't get past the first diner. Naftly demanded a Western omelet, donuts, rolls, coffee and cigarettes. At the airlines freight building, Junior unlocked the doors and told Naftly to turn on some light switches. Naftly walked around like an official. He came back and lit a cigarette.

The boss said he didn't care who came to work with Junior, as long as Junior was there to work. For the last year and a half, Junior has brought his father to work. The son gave the father packages to put in the bin for Madrid. Then he told Naftly to go back and check on it. Naftly walked with shoulders squared and chin high. I pass this test. The Iceland bin was next. After work now and then, Junior took the father around to the Owl Tavern, where Junior had a beer, the father a soda; since the fall, the father no longer likes the taste of beer.

At home, Junior goes out with girls at night and his mother takes care of Naftly.

And then after a day in which Naftly had successfully checked two bins, Junior and his mother were in the kitchen when they heard Naftly suddenly laughing at the cartoon show.

When I stopped around to see them, Junior asked, "Your brain operation, when do you get it?"

"Tuesday."

"I'm from the old generations. I'm the only son. I take care of my father. Your family is old style, right?"

"I guess so."

"If your operation is bad for you, somebody in your family just takes you out someplace every day," he said.

I looked at the back of the father's head. His short brown hair was there and nothing else. I touched the back of the head. The guy didn't even have a bump. Nothing showed.

But nowhere can any of them see the

secret of the brain, and that is consciousness.

Nobody can explain where consciousness comes from because nobody knows the first thing about it. How can they? The exclusive opportunity to give you consciousness resides with a higher power. That is what I believed when I came into this, and a furious search produced nothing to make me change.

Instead of being intimidated by the books, I simply went along as if I were working on the sports desk of the *Press* newspaper, handling high school baseball stories from stringers. A story would say Bryant High had defeated Long Island City by 4–3. The box score was on a separate sheet. You added up the box score to make sure that Bryant had four runs and Long Island City three, after which you checked the box score for names mentioned in the story to make sure the heroics were recorded. Then you checked the line score, the inning by inning.

That pencil stopped dead if you found only three Bryant runs in the box score instead of the four in the story. Of course a pencil for corrections. A thick black newsroom pencil. My friend Norman Mailer was saying one day that he couldn't imagine correcting anything without a pencil. No question. Anything electronic glides. It may be good for spotting errors by others, but if you want to correct your own errors, and impress on yourself the doctrine of imperfection, then the pencil must stop dead and be raised and then come down again and be pushed as you write. Sharp, tedious motions. Thus heightening the error and placing your senses even more on the alert for whatever was next. In the case of a wrong baseball score, there was an immediate yell for the stringer who wrote it.

Which is how I looked through this pile of books and papers on the brain. I looked for the word *consciousness* because it is here that science and religion walk away from each other and I go with religion. I will go into an operating room clutching good peasant beliefs of soul and heaven and hell. I expect that at the last minute, so does most everybody else.

Still, my eyes riveted on those passages about consciousness. And one exalted name after another delivered preposterous theories. Plato said that men made semen in their heads. Nobody called him on it and his notion lasted fifteen hundred years. Aristotle thought the quintessential air of life went to the heart, and the brain cooled the blood. That went on for eight or nine centuries. Galen said that all of life came from the humors in the blood. Phlegm formed the phlegmatic person; the black bile, also known as melancholy, made men vile. The yellow bile caused irritability. And deep in an artery was the sanguine fluid. He decided that humans had a rational soul in the brain, the animal soul in the heart. I'll tell you that right there I began to search the pages for more. I thought of one searing day at Chu Lai in Vietnam, where there were many dead on orange sand and beside a motionless South China Sea. A Marine lieutenant from the Bronx with an Irish name, who had just spent so long cold with fear and shrieking in the ecstasy of gunfire, stood in the sun and the dead and said, in the same words and emotion from the heart as I guess they have used for thousands of years, "This is every man's game."

Therefore, Galen had a notion worth studying, but I read on, and asked others who had studied, and there was no further indication that he had a belief that went beyond the statement. Nor did he say where the soul in the brain came from.

Descartes saw one soul, in the pineal gland in the brain, acting as a third eye.

These thoughts lasted through many centuries, one immortal thinker after the other, making pronouncements that ran from the bizarre to such murkiness as not to be explainable anywhere. If they were around today on the Internet, they would have the whole of civilization totally insane.

There are many books written about consciousness now, all aimed first at bookstores and reviewers, each shipment of them leaping out of the carton with head fakes. Had I understood that the study of neurobiology is only ten years old, that these people at colleges and universities are as vulnerable as anybody else to the numbing, dazzling temptation of a bestseller, and going beyond this, to the acclaim of people in science all over the world, had I known that, then I never would have kept on turning pages that were as heavy as cement slabs.

I had two things I wanted to know at this moment of my life:

When they operate, does that mean that the knife goes into my mind, too, or are the mind and brain separate? Or, if they are somehow intimately connected, can you still assist one part that is ailing and leave the rest alone?

The second question is, What is consciousness and where does it come from? And that remains the entire game.

Today's people listed as scholars announce a search for consciousness, and then they come up with fascinating evidence of how our actions are shaped by evolution, by the needs of people in prehistoric times to get through the day. Freezing in terror is our inheritance from people who lived in jungles and saved their lives by being frightened motionless as animals the size of apartment buildings tried to find them.

These passages were fine to read, but then the old copyreader in me checked the box score. Consciousness does not score a run.

I tried climbing over stony sentences purportedly about consciousness and could find nothing. One Sunday I was dazzled by the front page of the *Times* newspaper book review which said a book by a West Coast professor, Churchland, was a work of such scope that the author clearly was a gigantic figure. I hope so. I had great difficulty in reading what he was writing about. You do not need a complex sentence to deliver a complex thought. He said that there is no mind to begin with, that you are a fool to believe that you have one, that the mind is an illusion. Everything is in a solid brain. He put a label on one belief as "Vitalist." The "Vitalist" believes that a spark of life from God causes things to be living. Of course he regarded this as a belief that was held by people who were every bit as ignorant as his wife's biology teacher. He wrote that biological life is an intricate but purely physical phenomenon. Churchland writes, "Might consciousness have a similar fate in store?" He noted that people are so slow in learning anything about consciousness that he was in despair of ever understanding consciousness at all.

I go to the box score on his book and the pencil stops dead. The book says it will tell me about consciousness and when I go to the box score again, it reads the same: Consciousness does not score.

In one crowded, thrilling part of the city, at New York University around Washington Square Park, on the streets of the young, was the school's Glimcher Laboratory. In one room, a monkey sat on a stool inside a high glass box. He could move any part of his body, but he had this connection around his neck.

"An electrode," Paul Glimcher explained. "A one-quarter of a thousandth of an inch electrode. We have a thin hair in the brain." Glimcher is in his early thirties. He is short and thin and has close-cropped black hair. Much of his cheeks and chin is covered by a deep black beard. He wears green drawstring lab pants.

The monkey works his mouth on a plug that is at the end of a plastic tube coming down from a wall container that is filled with a fluid.

"Hawaiian Punch," Glimcher says. "Monkeys love it. That's the reward if he does the experiment right."

The monkey now is working even harder on the plug. "They have some way of breaking the seal sometimes so they get the Hawaiian Punch without doing the experiment," Glimcher says.

If there is one thing we know from the start about the monkey's brain, it is that it is crooked.

The monkey in the glass box faced a black light board on a wall. One small bulb, of flashlight size, came on. Now several spaces to the right and higher up, a small bulb went on. A small bulb went on well below it. If the light in the center turns red, the monkey is supposed to remember to look up at the top light. If he does, Hawaiian Punch flows into his mouth. If the light in the center turns green, the monkey's recall should tell him to look down if he wants the reward.

The wire in the monkey's brain recorded the activity of a single nerve cell. That reaction, in red and green lines, ran across

188

one screen. The hope is to capture exactly what happens to the cell at the instant of thought. Glimcher pushed a button to make the light green. The monkey looked down at the light bulb that was low. Suddenly his face lit up more than any bulb. The Hawaiian Punch reward was flooding into his greedy little mouth. Then the juice stopped.

Glimcher then turned the light in the center red. This time the monkey looked up and the mouth plug turned sweet again.

"So he remembers things," I said to Glimcher.

"Yes."

"Where is the memory in his brain?"

"Pretty much everywhere."

The sample of one cell is useful in a laboratory but Glimcher said that if it was going to advance anything he needed to work with 100,000 cells.

"You can show a segment of consciousness making a decision now," he said. "We can get a flow diagram of what happens when the monkey sees something and acts on it. This is free will in a monkey. This is free choice in a monkey. But a wiring diagram is the best anybody can do now. We're about forty years away from finding important answers."

Glimcher said the monkey experiment is

part of one strategy of measuring the way the brain works. "Another is by neuro imaging. Images are taken with MRIs and PET scans. You've seen an MRI. The PET scan is another way to image. You inject fluid. You take images of a person with his eyes closed, and then have him open his eyes and see a pattern of checkerboards. This causes about a million brain cells to move around. As he watches the checkerboard, the measure of blood in the brain shows the local region that the retina reaches.

"However, that strategy needs one million neurons at a time to tell what is happening. That places a strong limit as to how the brain uses something, but it does show what location is reached. The imaging also is done on somebody watching a display of numbers, but is told to ignore thinking about them. Just stare. Then the person is asked to concentrate on the numbers and add up columns of them. The difference between not thinking of the numbers and then working on them shows up in the part of the brain that uses arithmetic."

"What part is that?" I asked, figuring if it's numbers, I don't need it.

"It lights up everywhere," he said. "They say that they have great localization with these experiments. They do. It is localized in the frontal cortex. There are only one billion neurons there.

"What you do in this strategy is have somebody not do something, then have him do it and take a picture of each thing and then subtract one from the other and get the difference."

You leave his laboratory and are left with writings that became nebulous and piled words that have no meaning when they come to the spirit. Where does a personality come from? What is a personality anyway? What is a sense of humor? Where do these powers live in the brain? Nobody knows. You are not alive without them and nobody knows the first thing about them. They have no anatomical evidence for so much of what they say, although I wish they did because I am terrific if I have some facts to go through, even the worst jumble of facts, and could find out what to anticipate and fear. When I am working on something with more than one or two strands to it, there always comes a point in the writing when it becomes chaotic and I think all is lost and there is great anxiety and I suddenly panic and become too tired to think or write. Then the thing suddenly explains itself in the writing of it. I don't know if I do it in thinking, but I certainly do it in writing. Now, in trying to find out what can happen to my mind in an operation, I came upon no list of facts and long passages on consciousness to go through and write about. They all have a theory and it is not real and they don't even have a Bible.

In my present position, my brain about to be on an operating table, I say I'm right and I lead with a prayer, if you don't mind.

I take my leap away from science. The left chamber of the brain carries numbers and the alphabet. The right chamber of the brain sees in pictures. But you didn't come into the world with the numbers or the alphabet in your head. We have only twenty-six letters. The Chinese have ten thousand characters. Certainly, they weren't born with them. So these things must be taught.

The area of the brain that gives you body movements, appetite, the need for warmth and shelter, can be found at the start of the spinal cord.

But where does love come from? Where do you get allegiance and loyalty? Who told you of the virtues to preserve society? Isn't there an unconscious pull for a person to want to try to help, and then a pull to make life better for himself first? Wouldn't it be a sin if the individual places his wants, greed mostly, as being more important than society? It is right here, at the mention of sin, that a force is in charge. A force that is not present on any test. The belief in it is a couple of thousand years old and I picked it up in a classroom and church in Queens and I carried it with me this far, and there is not the slightest chance that anything can change. You are baptized, raised, die and get buried as a Catholic. This unseen rule, power, force, immutable belief cannot be found with electricity. They will search for years, through the hundreds and hundreds of millions of wires that make up the brain. They will find nothing. Unless they want to look for a higher power and that higher power has the exclusive opportunity to create and run the world and to give those in it the gift of consciousness.

The El train the color of rust runs through all my beginnings. I am riding it from Queens to Manhattan. Past these old ornate buildings on Jamaica Avenue that doze in the sunlight patterns coming through the tracks. This is a Friday. I have Saturday. Then I have Sunday. Early Monday, I get a plane to Phoenix and if I get back, we'll see how much I can think about anything.

Now, on the Jamaica Avenue below is the street of my first job, my first love. The train goes past movie houses and bank buildings that always were the pilings for the people living on these streets.

Now they might be even stronger. They are musty gospel arenas where ministers shout and women call out:

"Lord HEAR us!"

The train runs past the temporal: wheezing five-story houses with women staring from top-floor windows that are eye level with the train. Arms folded, they inspect the train and the air it stirs. Abruptly, the nose of the train goes up, and below spreads the plaza of the Williamsburg Bridge and then the bridge and its gray towers and cables rise, and across the river these buildings blazing with sun climb high out of Manhattan's financial streets. The buildings are gone as the train suddenly dives down and rushes around a curve and then comes up again. Bridge, river, harbor, buildings, sky spinning in your eyes. Up, up, up goes the train and everything behind has vanished, all I ever wanted or ever knew, all the failures, fortune, mistakes, accidents, successes, and now there is only the spinning sky.

And then the train drops flat onto the trackbed. Going across the bridge you look straight down, and the river shows through the planks. Ahead are the buildings, the soot, the rude, thrilling crowded blocks of downtown New York. Yet it is the healthiest city in the world. The people are so used to walking many blocks each day, and are in the vortex of the nation's health information, that the average New Yorker weighs five or six pounds less than people in the rest of America, where they eat fried grease and the farther they live from a city the less walking they do. A most common American sight is that of a fat slob male bundled up in a down jacket and so wedged into the front of his pickup truck that he has to struggle to get in and out. In Manhattan every day, the thin come in regiments up the subway steps.

On the banks of the East River was the old sand-colored stone fortress that took so much of my energy when I worked there. It was a Hearst paper, the *New York Journal-American*, a newspaper where even the weather report was suspect; the masthead of the paper should have read:

William R. Hearst Jr., Publisher.

Paul Schoenstein, Managing Editor.

George Brown, Chief Shylock.

Georgie Brown was more important to the paper than the copyreaders. He had so much business that the paper formalized his role in daily journalism and gave him an office on the fourth floor. He had nothing else to do. They didn't even make him read the paper. He was the shylock and as a convenience to shylock and customers, the plant manager gave Georgie an office. It was better than having crowds pushing around the press room and somebody winding up with his hand going through the roller and coming out on page one.

There was a Beneficial Finance Company office on 33rd Street and Seventh Avenue and a Household Finance office around the corner on 34th Street. The limit was $500 for twenty-four months. At first what I'd do is borrow the $500 from Beneficial and when I got behind in payments, which was right away, I went around to Household and borrowed from them so I could pay Beneficial. The roof would collapse when you couldn't make the payment either to Beneficial or to Household. I was supposed to be trying a first novel. Instead I was taking two days at a time to borrow the rent. It costs you your life to be broke.

One day at the *Journal-American* sports desk, David Anderson handed me the phone. He winds up a famous sportswriter for the *Times* newspaper, but from the very start he was such a legitimate guy that he couldn't tell it was a creditor on the phone. I picked up the phone. "This is Mr. Peters from Beneficial." All Beneficial Finance people were Mr. Peters.

"Just a minute, I'll get him."

I hung up. He called back. But by now, Lew King, who knew all there was about being broke, was covering the phones like a shortstop. "That fellow is in Pittsburgh covering the Dodgers and Pirates game."

Afterwards, a Mr. Fiore from Household, all Household people were named Fiore, called. "Where in Pittsburgh is Mr. Breslin?" he asked King.

"I didn't tell you he was there," King said. "Besides, he's in Detroit for the Tigers and Yankees game."

That the Household guy mentioned me being in Pittsburgh was all the proof we needed that they were in collusion.

"At least Georgie Brown doesn't tell anybody," Lew King said.

That is how we went from week to week, and it seemed as if it would never end. I wasn't alone. I didn't know anybody who had forty dollars. All we had was trouble because of freaking money.

I am the only man in North America who not only cannot drive but also has had his car repossessed twice.

Hardly anybody knows what the word *repossess* means anymore. They don't know anybody anymore who is that openly broke that the bank or the finance company takes the car back. That happens all the time in black and Hispanic neighborhoods, but most people know nothing of such calamities.

My memory does. I cannot recall a single solitary thing about the day my bank account showed a million dollars. But I know the hour-by-hour of the car being repossessed in Baldwin, Long Island. It is no big deal to recount foolish blunders. Everybody tells the truth now and then. What you have to learn is that the foolishness is committed by a fool.

My wife went into the garage in Baldwin to get the station wagon out to drive the kids someplace one morning. She came back in yelling, "Somebody stole the car!" While she was going to the phone, she asked me, "Did you make the payment?"

"Certainly," I said. I sure had not. Not this last payment, nor the two payments before that. Or was it three payments before the last one I missed? I don't know. They sent a letter and I did exactly what I was supposed to do: I threw it out. Then I threw out the rest of the mail that came with it. You should do that with all your mail every day; nothing good ever comes in the mail.

My wife was on the phone excitedly telling police that the car had been stolen when she stopped and said, "Oh." She hung up and said to me, "It's repossessed by the National City Bank." Her voice was wounded, and at the same time cold. The moment the house was empty, she started firing grape and canister at me.

It took me two days to get the car back. I had to borrow the money from a saloon owner, Mutchie, and my friend at work, Lew King, who first had to go borrow from George Brown. I went to the bank's car finance office and waited an hour and a half because the guy was out to lunch. Afterward, I went over the bridge to the garage in Brooklyn where they stored repossessed cars. Of course I can't drive so I had to ask my friend Danny from the newspaper cityroom for help. He couldn't come until the next day. He brought along a big guy who was a friend of his. When I got the car out of hock, Danny drove me home and the big guy followed Danny and then took him home to Brooklyn. I had to pay late charges on the car payment, buy drinks in Mutchie's bar, where I borrowed the money, then pay Danny to drive the car. It costs you money to be broke.

And now, the way it works, I am on Fifth

Avenue in Brooklyn one day a lot of years after this and I was a big shot on the loose; saying hello to a guy in front of his store, then to two women on the corner who knew me, returning a wave to a cabdriver. Good boy yourself, Breslin, you're doing good. I swing into this firehouse for coffee. I go sideways against the wall and slide along the polished old pumper and go into the kitchen. Two guys in T-shirts look up from their home improvement magazines and say hello.

"Want coffee?" a guy in the kitchen area says.

"Why do you think I'm here?" I say it without looking at the guy.

Handing me the coffee he says, "You knew a friend of mine, Danny. I went with him one time out to your house. You had some kind of trouble with your car." He was a big pleasant guy with a nice memory he could lose.

While it may not have looked that way, I always had my future in my two typing fingers. When I started to get out, I had a magazine article to do, for decent money, too, on James Donovan, the Brooklyn lawyer involved in a spy swap with Russia. David Wise, the fine Washington writer, told me to try the guy. Donovan had been the lawyer for Russian spy Rudolph Abel. The Russians had Gary Powers, a spy pilot shot down in his U-2 plane over Russia. The trade was made on a bridge between West and East Berlin. Abel never even had told Donovan, or anybody else, his right name or what he did for a living. Donovan loved him for that. As Donovan walked off the bridge, he looked at Powers, who did not appear to be too heroic, and then said, "This is a very bad deal for the United States of America."

I wrote the story all weekend. When I turned it in on Monday, the editor liked it so much that he raised the fee to $2,500 instead of the $1,500 I was supposed to get.

I heard that, I said freak you. I didn't even have the money yet, but I felt like I did.

Let me see them turn off the lights.

I had it wrong. By the time I got home, they had absolutely turned off the gas.

I kept going. For my first book, *Can't Anybody Here Play the Game?*, I was scheduled on *The Tonight Show* in May of 1963. At five I was in a bar on the ground floor of 30 Rockefeller Center. I had one drink with Ed McMahon, the *Tonight Show* announcer, and went up with him to tape the show. Johnny Carson, trumpets and applause. The big time.

When we got home, here was the next-door neighbor, Annette Kirschenbaum, sitting in our kitchen with two candles.

"They shut your electricity off," she said. "If you were here you wouldn't have been able to see yourself on the show."

She shook her head. "You'll be like this forever."

I was not. But I did not forget the physical reaction that is caused by a shortage of cash. Still, today, my nose twitches when it comes anywhere near somebody with no money. The guy can be dressed like a Swiss Guard, but if he has no money my nose quivers and that means look out for him, tunic and all he's a broker. Let me tell you about my momentary intoxicating brush with the great publishing magnate Robert Maxwell from Great Britain. He bought the *New York Daily News* newspaper. I was at this time at another paper, *Newsday.* In bed in the morning I read an interview in the *Times* newspaper in which Maxwell said his first order of business was to bring back Jimmy Breslin to the *News.* I sat bolt upright. On the television was the Channel 5 morning program and they were billboarding an up-coming live interview with Maxwell on his yacht, then tied up at 23rd Street in the

East River. Now I will show you how I use my years in my city as my own private, inside information alley. I called the control room at Channel 5 and got my friend Gail Yancosek, the morning show's producer. I know her for twenty-five years. I yelled, "Mention my name!" She talked into the earpiece of the reporter, Dick Oliver, who was on the yacht, waiting to go on. I had worked with Oliver and together we spent at least three full years at the bar. Now when the interview got going, Oliver brought up my name. And on live television, Fat Robert Maxwell looked directly into the camera and said, "If Lord Breslin is within hearing, his Lordship should be advised that money never stands in the way of people of our caliber."

I was in bed, and I stuck another pillow behind my head and I said, "I think I'll stay home today and smell the money!"

My friend Peter Johnson and I went to lunch with him at the hotel Carlyle. Right away, Maxwell said, "Do you have a contract?" I said, yes. He said, "Well, we've seen these things before, haven't we? I am going to give you a million dollars to come to the *Daily News*. We can work out the yearly salary details with Mr. Johnson here at our leisure."

He was infuriated when I told him that I no longer drank. He had two or three vodkas. Johnson remembers three. Then he had a bottle of white wine. He said that he was opening a national Thoroughbred racing daily paper the next day to compete with Rupert Murdoch. After that, a big cold beer. He drained it. His head dropped onto his chest and he started snoring. He woke up and had two big brandies and coffee.

When the waiter brought the check, he gave it to Maxwell. There was a pause. Maxwell eyed the table. But this is impossible, I told myself. Is he looking for one of us to take the check? Of course he is.

First, I brushed my fingertips against my nose in an attempt to stop it from quivering. It only became worse. Broke. I am supposed to get a million dollars for myself off this man and I keep getting the scent of a busted-down valise. Finally, I had to run the back of my right hand across the nose to calm it. With a certain display of weariness, Maxwell went into his pocket. He brought out cash. It was a lot of pocket cash, I guess, but there was no credit card and he didn't even attempt to sign the check and let the house bill him. Was he afraid of a waiter's rebuff? I hadn't been in the Carlyle hotel in some time but I could have signed that check and the hotel would have been delighted.

We shook hands. He looked at Johnson. "We shall be in touch about the necessary arrangements."

Johnson and I went outside and stood on Madison Avenue.

"Peter, could this guy be broke? What am I asking you for? I know he's broke. I grew up with this in the air."

"The hotel wouldn't let him sign," Peter said.

Afterward, whenever I saw or heard his name, I had a whiff of Man Broke. Is it my opinion that provokes this response, or is it caused by actual fact? I settled that by staying clear of the famous international publishing magnate. He was so fantastically brazen that on television, he had Dinkins the mayor and Cuomo the governor calling him "Sir Robert." I yelled at the screen: "He got the title from the same place where he gets his money." He then went over the side of his yacht off the Canary Islands. Of course he had nothing and had been raiding the pension funds of workers at one of his papers, the London *Mirror*. He left his two sons as defendants in criminal court in London.

So in my life as an American worker I

went from being a penniless copyboy to discovering a publisher who comes up empty. And maybe finding him at the end of my run. Nobody ever told me that life could be this fast. I lived in the everyday excitement of meeting strangers who unfold in front of you and become people you cannot wait to tell others about. How can you be expected to notice what is happening to your own life? I am supposed to be sitting on the copyboys' bench, feet kicking, smoking cigarettes, saying to Mickey the girl clerk, Want a screw? and now suddenly I look down and see that my feet are pawing strange dirt at the lip of a grave that maybe could be mine. And that is blinding speed.

Anybody old can tell you how fast the last years go. I only heard one person ever say anything about how early speed burns up the ground before you can set foot on it.

I was walking out of Arlington Cemetery after Jack Kennedy's funeral and my friend Mary McGrory, the columnist, said to Pat Moynihan, now a New York senator, "We'll never laugh again."

And Moynihan said, "Oh, of course we'll laugh again, Mary. It's just that we won't be young again."

Who listened?

We fetch news each day of accidents and

arrogance, of dancing and drama, fire and fame, lies and love, mayhem and murder. Nobody brings news of your own death.

The El train I was riding was across the bridge and became a subway. I got off at City Hall. While I walked by, I suddenly saw my days spent in the spring of 1969. Norman Mailer and I, both between books, entered the Democratic mayoralty primary. We were at Brooklyn College, with the crowd so big they had to put us into two auditoriums, and we shuttled back and forth. Once we were in the same place and a student asked, "There was a huge amount of snow in Queens last winter and the mayor didn't get it cleaned up. What would you do if there was a big snowstorm and you were the mayor?"

Mailer stepped forward.

"Sir, I'd piss on it."

While they laughed uproariously, they never considered that it was precisely what everybody should have been saying about the snow in Queens, which was irrelevant; what the people really wanted was to make the blacks go away.

I walked past the police building, which was behind City Hall, and right away, I saw the lights blazing on the bald spot on the top of David Berkowitz's head on the night they caught him. A lunatic with a gun that worked every time. He killed five young women with long dark hair and one young man and wounded seven others.

They have him handcuffed to a chair in a large office. He sees me in the doorway and he says to Timmy Dowd, the inspector, "That's Jimmy Breslin. He's a very good friend of mine."

He calls himself "Son of Sam" and says Sam is a black dog inside his head. He says that the dog is a thousand years old. I wondered if they opened up Berkowitz's head, would the dog bite the surgeon's hand?

At least he didn't say that God had told him to kill people. Every assassin and serial killer says, in a voice throbbing with voodoo, that God told him to kill. Like any strong insanity, Berkowitz's swirled in the air and touched so many, with one event slapping into the next. His nickname stayed in the ear, and he was a mixture of voodoo, idiot and desperate, eerie danger. He had worked as a zip code checker in the Bronx Post Office, where a woman working as a mail sorter was in love with him. He slept on the floor of a studio apartment in Yonkers on a green blanket with "Marijuana" in gold stitching. This was in 1977 and I was living in the section of Queens called Forest Hills

Gardens. He killed one young woman, Christine Freund, five blocks from my house. Five weeks later, at virtually the same spot, Virginia Voskeriechian, walking from the subway after classes at Barnard College in Manhattan, had a gunman suddenly crouch in front of her. She held a thick textbook against her face. He put the gun against the textbook and shot. She fell dead and he ran away. Both murders were done with the same gun, a .44 Bulldog.

My friend Detective Andy Camera drew Virginia Voskeriechian's chalk outline on the sidewalk. She had only excellent marks in school as a record of her life lived when death surprised. I stared at the chalk and thought of all that she could have done that we would never know. I could hear her children laughing as they walked with her to the school around the corner. I used to walk my kids to school on this same sidewalk. There were hedges and on the other side of the hedges, pine needles. I wrote one column about this, for my newspaper, the *New York Daily News*. Then a letter came that was printed in pen in the hand of a ghost, with large eerie back-slanted letters. It said: "Hello from the cracks of the sidewalks in New York City and from the ants that grow in those cracks and feed on the dried blood of the dead that has settled into the cracks. . . ." He signed it "Son of Sam."

Only Murray Kempton, a columnist, said this dark, chilling power was not genius at all, but words hurled out of a deranged mind. He was right, as Berkowitz showed later. He wrote to me from the Kings County Hospital prison psychiatric ward, with a basket of lithium in him, and it was in high school longhand, not his famous slanted printing: "How are you? I see that the politicians want to use my head like a football."

But in the middle of that summer of 1977, the Son of Sam emptied many streets with each shooting. In Queens, Bronx and Brooklyn neighborhoods, there was an air of danger coming out of the commonplace, a front walk, a hedge, from behind a tree.

"You're my big hope," Timmy Dowd told me. "We're going to get him when he comes looking for you."

"That's great. Maybe I could get shot."

"I know you're a good citizen and you'll help us," Dowd said.

I preferred voting.

This mad dog also was shooting in the middle of a mayoralty election. In the middle of the night on a dark Queens side street, with two young people shot in a parked car and on the way to the hospital, with despair diffused about the small crowd around the car, Timmy Dowd had a hopeless tone in his voice. "All these nights trying to get this guy." And here you go in the morning, the candidate for reelection, Beame, after another comfortable night, stood in a large room in City Hall that had paintings on the wall and said that he was going to catch Son of Sam!

I decided, what with the killings near my house and the letter to me, that this guy knew where I lived. I would have moved heaven and earth to get my family out of his way. They went to my sister-in-law's house in Westhampton Beach. I went out there once, on a rainy Monday night. My wife and I sat in the window of an empty bar called Magic's on the main street in Westhampton. Cars went by slowly in the rain outside the window. Of course we didn't know what Berkowitz looked like or what kind of car he drove. I guess he saw us in the window all right when he drove by the bar that night, but the dog in his head, Sam, told him to go home because of the rain.

Berkowitz then shot a young woman named Stacy Moskowitz in Brooklyn. She died in Kings County Hospital on a hot Sunday morning. Detective Bill Clark came up to the gloomy rust-colored hospital with cake boxes from a bakery. They were for the nurses. He was your modern man: if he gave the nurse cookies, she would swiftly yank the slug from the victim's head. And he could be on his way with it to the crime lab.

It was the first time Clark and I ever spoke to each other; the sidewalk in front of Kings County became our Old School. Someday, the real Old School, the Ivy League, would carry him to the top of the sky.

This last shooting, of the young woman Stacy Moskowitz, took place in the 60th Precinct in Coney Island. A detective named John Fatico caught the case and began checking traffic summonses issued on the murder night. While Fatico was off-duty, a detective found one ticket issued to a car from Yonkers that had been parked illegally one block from the murder scene.

All the detectives from the 60th Precinct were diving into cars for the ride to Yonkers and perhaps fame just as Detective John Fatico arrived for work. Somebody yelled to him, "We're going for coffee. You watch the phones." Long ago Fatico learned that greed supersedes murder. They were stealing his case in his face! He jammed into one of the cars.

On the dashboard of Berkowitz's car parked on the street in Yonkers was a letter written in Berkowitz's deranged hand, instantly known to all. When Berkowitz came out to his car, they put a gun to his head and the Son of Sam case was over.

During the night in police headquarters, Berkowitz said he had been out hunting in Westhampton Beach, in Suffolk County, but went home because the dog had something against rain. Bill Clark came out of the room and gave me the date. I called my wife. Yes, it was my one night in Westhampton. If it did not rain that night, then this insane insect could have shot us. Could have? Who else was he looking for?

When I came back, Berkowitz was in the catacombs, under arrest for serial murders and unavailable for my personal inquiry. Instead at dawn here was Beame the mayor, standing shoulder-high between these big cops. Just as he had promised the voters, he had caught Son of Sam!

And Dick Schaap and Bill Clark and I went up to the NBC studios for the *Today* show. "Talk to this guy," I said to Jane Pauley. "Detective Bill Clark, Son of Sam squad. This is the guy that broke the case."

The camera's red light went on. Bill Clark fixed his big blue eyes on the camera's red light as, slowly, then increasingly faster, the formation of his brain changed. No longer did he think of himself as a police officer who was a doorman at a bar for extra money. Now he was a star.

The rest is details. One day in 1992, David Milch, who had taught literature at Yale and now was in television, called Michael Daly, the writer, who had gone to Yale. Milch wanted a New York City detective to work on a show he was trying to develop called *NYPD Blue.* Daly gave him Clark's number.

At this time, Clark lived in two rooms on the ground floor of a house on 16th Street in Brooklyn. He had two parrots who screamed, "Call the police! Call the police!" He now is in a big house in Santa Monica and might be the most successful ex-detective in New York police history in that he supervises scripts, and most successfully, on an enormous television hit.

6

On this last Sunday in New York before flying to Phoenix, I was about to leave for church in the morning when my wife said she wanted to come with me. Rather than changing affiliation, she was just providing company. That was nice of her, lend her presence.

Suddenly, in church the two fears that had been at first vague, their threat fleeting, presented themselves in their entirety. One was death, and I rejected that right there. Not that I am so bold and brave, but I am so used to hearing the word every day in work that it loses its threat. I am as sure as the night is dark that I will turn white with the frost of fear at the end. So sure that I hoped I would be able to keep my mouth shut and not whimper aloud.

If you fear you are going to die, you start suffering the moment you start being afraid. That would come, I was sure, but I could certainly wait.

The second fear was the one that was real

to me, and that was of surviving the operation all right, heart and lungs fine, but still coming out of it with some degree of being a zombie.

That would leave so many in my family in the worst possible condition, that of being subjugated to the illness.

I barely could handle the thought of that. I have children I started to love fiercely the moment I found out I had a threat in my head. Once, I loved them without a thought, it was just a natural feeling. Now the thought of them caused pangs. If I passed, I said to myself, using the word from black neighborhoods, an expression out of the old South that is usually lost in a populace that only wants to speak of health care, I hoped that they wouldn't be able to figure out who I was to begin with. I had some theory that if I remained half a mystery, it would be easier for all of mine to get over me. There have been many Jimmy Breslins because of all the people I identified with so much, turning me into them, or them into me, that I can't explain one Jimmy Breslin. There is only one thing constant about me, that I cannot stand criticism or compliments. Otherwise, I've been hiding from my feelings for so long and becoming part of what I see that I wonder what my feelings are, and why I'm always afraid of them.

It was all right at the start of this Sunday mass. I knelt, she sat. She stood up, along with everybody in the church, for the Gospel. Doesn't the priest get no more than three sentences into reading it, and he is saying something about Jews. I don't know what he read exactly, but it certainly wasn't leading anywhere except to the fact that the Jews killed Christ. I don't know where it was in the Gospel because by this time the shock was in my vasticulars, and I wasn't sure of what I was hearing. He then continued these thoughts in the sermon. The whole sermon. Beautiful. He pointed out that in the fabric of life the Jews and Catholics were interwoven. That freaking fabric again. What kind of fabric is it, worsted? Gabardine? If he said one more time "Catholics and Jews" or "Christians and Jews" just to make sure we all knew that there was a difference, and that the difference was that the Jews killed Christ, I knew I was going to be faced with a choice: leave with her or sit alone. The priest brought up the Jews again. Twice in a row, I think. I put my head down and waited for it to end.

"Absolutely," she said on the sidewalk. "There's no chance."

"For you?"

"No, for the Catholics. The first thing they do is separate them. They're Catholics and the Jews killed Christ. Or Christians. They use that word when they get tired of saying Catholic. But they never change the other part of it. Jews. The Jews killed Christ. They teach that in grammar school. What chance do their kids have? Why wouldn't they run around beating us up? When I grew up, we never went east of Broadway. It was very bad between Broadway and Central Park West. All Irish. Good and Irish. I used to hate to go visit my cousins, the Luckstones. They lived on 89th and Central Park West. I walked to 86th Street. Big street. You were safe from the Irish. That was when I was in grammar school. So here we are all these years later and they're saying the same thing. All the Jews killed Christ. I'm sure they say it every Sunday. How many Jews did the killing? Millions? There was a lynch mob and if you go to church you'll hear them saying I was part of it."

We walked in silence.

"I'm sorry, dear, but that was the last time for me," she said.

Usually, I ignore totally the words and rules of this church. Most of the cardinals of the Catholic Church come from Italy and that is temporary insanity. Yet I cannot get out of the habit of going to church to pray. I know that you need no stone building to pray for your life. Besides, the churches have interiors that are gloomy without end and I choose to believe in the marriage at Cana, where the Lord made wine out of water to keep the reception going. Why can't we reflect some of that joy in Queens? I know that I was at a pope's funeral in Rome and the day before the ceremony I was inside St. Peter's and an arm waved vigorously from the narrow spiral staircase that winds under the altar and to the tunnels below. The arm belonged to Hugh Carey, who was in Rome as the governor of New York. It was a most urgent wave. I went to the stairs, pushed my way down and there at the very bottom was Hugh Carey at a small public bar.

"They've put the fun back in whiskey!"

His finger made a circle in the air and the bartender reached for a bottle. By the third drink we were the only ones in Rome extolling the late pope, whose mourners mostly had eyes as dry as sand.

There can be only good from churches in New York giving women, who make up most of the worshippers, a glass of sherry or so in the foyer to send them home filled with holiness and cheer.

Still, my past memory causes me to need a church, as gloomy as they are.

Later that Sunday afternoon, my dentist, Arthur Guilder, came to his office to work on me to make sure no filling falls out while I'm in an operation and they have to cut my throat open to keep me from choking to death.

I pick up a science magazine in the waiting room and here is another story about how people lose their sense of smell if something happens to the brain. The article I am reading in the dentist's office is the same thing that I had heard before, that the olfactory nerve runs near the optic chiasm and that sits on the Circle of Willis, and that is where all my trouble with aneurysm happens to be, directly in front of the areas of the brain that hold the senses of smell and taste and I was virtually certain to lose these powers. So if there is damage to the olfactory nerve, which is not unusual in brain operations, then my sense of taste and smell would be less acute, if not totally absent. I have a smell in my mind that relates instantly to just about everything I've ever done. Mustard, early coffee and late coffee — they are different — fresh grass, which I don't like because that means sunlight and I like rain, and the musty smell that was sour but at the same time with an off-sweet taste of licorice. It was printer's ink and that first deep breath ran into my consciousness forever. Words are best when they have their start amidst the smells of printing.

After the visit to the dentist, I was walking home, going along Central Park South, and when I looked in the window at the place where it started, the Essex House Hotel on Central Park South, I smelled sweet vermouth. Here is Casey Stengel, just inside at this bar, with a Manhattan drink in his hand, insisting that I have one, too, and that vermouth is strong in my nose. He is saying, "These shocks are making my brain flake to pieces which at my age is no good and I ought to be gettin' out of here and, here, I'll have another one of these."

He is seventy-three on this day and he is a famous baseball man who has managed the New York Yankees of Joe DiMaggio, Mickey Mantle, Whitey Ford, and he winds up managing the first New York Mets baseball team that is the worst team in the history of all sports in the world. Maybe they are killing this old man but whether I realize it or not at this moment, they are about to make my life.

Marvin Throneberry mainly. Some people keep little mementos of their lives, a diploma, a note from the boss, an award. In my house there is a grotto to Marvin Throneberry. He was a baseball player out of Tennessee who had a reasonable major league career until he was sold to the Mets in time for their first year, and from the very first day all the devils from so many skies over baseball fields got inside that bald head and turned Marvin into a vivid comic athlete. It is remarkable that most people today would be familiar only with his light beer commercials. Because he filled the air of America with some of the last humor that sports has been able to give us. I always said that having Marvin Throneberry on your team was like having Willie Sutton work in your bank.

Marvin at this very moment is causing Stengel to wince at the Essex House bar. Earlier in the day, a Sunday, at the old Polo Grounds field in uptown Manhattan, I am sitting in the press box when I first see Stengel start to fall apart. Throneberry is at bat against the Chicago Cubs with two runners on and two out. He pulls the ball deep between the right and centerfielders. Both Mets runners race home. Throneberry, with wonderful running action, goes past first and second and slides into third base. The few people in the stands clap. In the dugout, Casey Stengel takes off his hat and waves it in congratulations.

The first baseman for the Chicago Cubs, who is Ernie Banks, has called for the baseball. He announces that Throneberry had not touched first base. The umpire, Dusty Boggess, screams, "Out!"

Throneberry is out, the runs don't count, the inning is over and the Mets lose the game by a full twelve runs.

Afterward, in the evening dusk, Stengel sat in an undershirt in the clubhouse in centerfield and calls to the clubhouse man, "Get that Throneberry in here."

Throneberry comes in, tying his tie. Stengel glares at him. "Leave me ask you something. Are you an adult?"

Throneberry doesn't answer.

"All my life," Stengel says, "I hear fellas tell stories about not touching first base. But it was only things that fellas told on train rides when you're drinking liquor or at some dinner when they wanted people to laugh.

"You just done it right in front of my very eyes. What the hell do you have to say for yourself?"

"Ah don't know why you're so excited," Throneberry says. "Ah never touched second, either."

Beautiful. There were two people in from

a bank in California and somebody else and me and we all went with Stengel by cab to barside, Essex House, where the others drop off after a couple of drinks and Stengel is ordering these stiff Manhattans with vermouth and whiskey and if he has one, he has a hundred. I have enough of them to lock my legs. It gets late of a Sunday night and the maintenance man is running a vacuum on the empty dining room. Stengel calls him over. But the man leaves the machine on so Stengel has to shout. "My fella at first which is Marvelous Marvin Throneberry. Out in St. Louis he is running a man down between first and second. The man runs away from Throneberry. Throneberry gets mad that he don't throw the ball to anybody. He is going to catch the man himself. Throneberry chases the man. And your Mister Musial just runs home and he is in the dugout and the game is over. Mister Throneberry is still chasing the runner.

"How do you like that?" Stengel yelled over the sound of the machine. The maintenance man had no answer. "He loses the game and he still doesn't tag the man out. Today he hits a triple which the umpire says 'Out!' which is like he did in St. Louis when he don't tag the man. Today he don't tag the base. First base. I got a man can't get

224

to first base on a triple! What do you think of that?"

Now Stengel says, "I'm shell-shocked. I'm not used to gettin' any of these shocks at all and now they come every inning. But you just spent all day writin' somethin' that winds up under the man's heel on the subway train tomorrow. You should write a book. Go home and write a book says Marvin Throneberry is marvelous. One biggest moron in the history of sports. Everybody readin' it will say, 'The fella is telling the truth. Marvin Throneberry is the one biggest moron ever to live.' "

I walked down to the E train home to Queens.

For me, one of the tests of a good idea is its ability to last through the hangover.

And this one did. I wrote a book about the Mets and Marvin Throneberry. While doing it, I am up to the scene of Stengel in the bar and I can hear something that he should have said that night, a wonderful thing that he should have said, so I figure that I will say it for him and the words are in his cadence. I just typed it out quick that Stengel said, "Sometimes you have to wonder, Can't Anybody Here Play This Game?"

It was a wonderful quote, and it made a tremendous book title. The title is so spontaneous that it springs off paper today just as it did the day that I made it up and typed it out. You see it somewhere every morning in titles over editorials, on the front page, on the sports pages, on the financial pages. Somebody on television always is saying it. It is somewhere in a league with things like *The Right Stuff* and *Catch-22* and *The Gang That Couldn't Shoot Straight* as titles most copied.

Then one morning I read a story that said they were putting together an off-Broadway play about baseball called *Can't Anybody* etc., and this time there is no delayed reaction. I came roiling out of that bed and grabbed the phone. I called my agent and screamed that we were getting robbed. He said, calmly, "Oh, you can't do anything about that. Casey Stengel said, 'Can't Anybody Here Play This Game.' That is his quote, remember? They are allowed to use his quote."

This happened on one other occasion. I was writing a column for the *Daily News* newspaper about somebody in City Hall making threats. I mentioned it to Burt Roberts, who was talking to me on the phone from the bench. He used to tell a witness to stop talking so he could take a phone call from a newspaper. Now he said he remembered Frank Hogan, the old district attorney, saying, "Beware of people who talk tough with a badge in their pocket. You usually find that there is something the matter with them inside." After telling me this, Burt hung up and let some poor murder defendant resume his story about how he did not kill this other guy, that he was just there on the same corner. I ran the Hogan quote in the story. It was good and it was sane. When Burt read it in the paper, he called. "When did Hogan tell you that?" I told him that he, Burt Roberts, was the source. "Hogan never said that to me," he said. About a year later, Roberts had a dinner program from the Frank Hogan Memorial, and here across the top of the program in thick black Gothic type was what the committee felt was the most meaningful quote of Hogan's long career: "Beware of people who talk tough. . . ." It made the newspapers and television and the large crowd of big shot New York people at the dinner was proud to be associated with such an inspiring title. It will appear next on the front of a new courthouse, with Burt Roberts making a long speech about it.

I guess I fought clear of the turmoil of all of us in near-success by stepping onto a private railroad car in Penn Station with

Mrs. Joan Payson, who owned the Mets. I was writing *Can't Anybody*. Still at this time, 1962, the trains had some of their style and they ran enough of them to Florida in the winter for the rich to have private cars on a train like this, the Florida East Coast Champion. The front half of the private car was a bedroom and the rear half was a parlor. Joan Payson was large and laughing and she was on a couch with stuffed pillows all around her and a poodle under her arm. A maid served me whiskey. Plenty of whiskey. I was quite stiff by Trenton and I got off the train in the night in Richmond, I think, reeling, and headed back to New York.

Then one thing goes right into another and her brother, John Hay Whitney, also known as Jock, came alongside me at the bar of the Artists and Writers restaurant on West 40th Street and says, "Can I buy a drink?"

Here at the bar, he stood with the first edition of his *Herald-Tribune* newspaper rolled up in the pocket of his tweed jacket. He owned the paper, which was in the building next to the bar. Now he asked me how I'd like to write for his newspaper. I had just come off working for Newhouse, Scripps-Howard and Hearst and you couldn't get paid from any of them and I was dead broke. I also was chesty with alcohol. I said, "After what I've been through you don't have enough money to pay me to go on a newspaper."

"I might," he said.

My friend Lew King kicked me. "He is fading you," King said.

Whitney was about the best of the rich. He had just been the ambassador to Great Britain. Better, he owned the Greentree Farms racing stable, which had meadows full of famous horses, including Tom Fool. He once got on a flight to Los Angeles with the galley proofs of a book that Samuel Goldwyn had turned down, saying, "Who wants a book about the Civil War? And about the losers yet?" He was financing David Selznick, the producer, and Selznick, too, hated the book. But a woman named Kay Brown, who worked as a story editor for Selznick, insisted the book would make a terrific movie. Whitney, who had the final vote because he had the fountain pen for the money, read the galleys. When the plane stopped for fuel in St. Louis, he sent a telegram to his partner in a film company, David Selznick: "SEND THE MITCHELL WOMAN FIFTY THOUSAND AS AN OPTION ON HER

BOOK. REGARDS. JOCK."

The book was called *Gone With the Wind*.

Then Whitney was saying, "My father died here in Manhasset, and I was in Oxford, and the butler called me at school. It was about eight at night. A fellow in the next room took the call out in the hall and told the butler, 'Hold on.' In the morning, I came back from the night in London and I walked by the phone and saw it hanging there. I picked it up and said, 'Hello.' And a voice said, 'Mister Whitney?' It was the butler in Manhasset. Then he said he had tragic news, that my father died. He said, 'I've been holding on for you for some time now.' There were only eight overseas lines at this time. We had one of them tied up for twelve hours waiting for me to come back from a night in London."

He said he used to fly by seaplane from Manhasset Bay to the East River, at the foot of Wall Street, when he had an investment company. "Everybody else started doing it and we stopped," he said. "Why be rich if everybody else does it?"

What he did was pay me the first good newspaper money given to anybody of my set. Everybody I knew came from nothing.

Now to the bar came a thin man who drank bourbon and smoked a dozen cigarettes. His name was James Bellows and he was the editor of the paper. He said he wanted me to start a new column. "What kind of a column?" I asked.

He answered with some writhing and a low voice. "Sort of like this," he said. He opened a paper to the first page of the second section. He put it on the bar and then took a thick old newspaper pencil and on the page he marked a space that was two columns wide and came down three quarters of the page. "You just sort of bring it up a level."

He had just spent some time in the office writhing over a thing he called "New York Magazine." It was to run in the Sunday paper. He had mumbled and waved a hand and Joseph Carter, who was to be the first editor, understood, although he couldn't catch a word of what was said.

Bellows had such an intensity about everybody except himself that people understood that his mumbling meant that he was convinced that they could do whatever it was that was supposed to be discussed, that he had picked them for this in the very first place.

So with absolutely no direction I invented a new form for news pages, a column based on something happening right now in this city. The column had to be made of conversations with people, and with word pictures of the places where they talked, and with insights into who the people were. The thing I did was to have people talk in a setting, and talk as humans actually do talk; nearly all quotes in a newspaper are lies because there isn't a human being alive who talks the way the papers quote them.

The television can be worse, because people talk like they're squid when they're being interviewed.

If people talk the way they do on television interviews or in newspapers, the world would drop dead of boredom.

Also, somewhere in the narrative there must be a place of enough strength for the column to rise from a bare straight story and, standing on stainless-steel legs of these quotes and scenes, become most informed commentary.

Forever before this, a newspaper column had consisted of straight opinion and was turned in a couple of days in advance. When you touched it in the paper, dust rose. You could read three paragraphs and throw it away because that is about all that was in any column.

Newspaper syndicates that sold columns sent them to newspapers by mail. This was to save telegraph costs. The biggest name columnists went out like common mail. Which was about all they were worth. Because of this the columns had to be done in advance. Once, Walter Winchell had a great crisis in his life when he telegraphed a column from Florida and a Hearst accountant charged him for the tolls. I was going to write my column right up against the deadline. I knew that Westbrook Pegler, who was the best newspaper columnist ever to live, until he became obsessed to the point of insanity with insulting Eleanor Roosevelt, told Murray Kempton one day, "You know the reason I went crazy? It wasn't Mizzus Roosevelt drove me that way. It was having to write on Monday for a Thursday paper."

I started off by doing five columns a week, of about 950 words.

I put in a column about Marvin the Torch telling a store owner that the blast that had just blown his dry goods store into the air was "nuclear." That started people talking out loud about how wonderful the column was. I went to Newark for the sentencing of Tony Provenzano, the Teamsters gangster. He sat with a huge diamond ring blazing in the courtroom light — my correlative object — as the judge gave him fifteen years for extortion.

Here you could see immediately why any success by an individual in this newspaper business must involve a strong publisher. This column on Provenzano was a very good column. Great. By itself, takes you nowhere. Garson Kanin and John O'Hara and people like that wrote letters to Jock Whitney saying how good it was, and, more important than making Breslin feel good, they extolled Whitney for having hired Breslin, thus putting them in great favor with Jock Whitney, and that never hurt.

I always walked a path that kept me at a good distance from miserable wretches in their suits and ties who bore the life out of you. It led me into the nearest hangout for Known Criminals. I then listened to their music. This is an important topic because I have decided that boring people are the true criminals. In a world where you live for about a minute and forty seconds, what right does anybody have to deaden one moment of time? If you can't laugh, if you can't give of yourself to others to liven their lives, then why don't you take your dead silence and go to jail with it where you belong?

Through the years when my job writing a column was new, I had in front of me each night marvelous groups of people, all openly dishonest. The shylock Ruby Stein spoke for all of them when a young woman, having a cigarette outside a funeral parlor during the wake of a slain accountant, asked him:

"And what business are you in, Mister Stein?"

Ruby's chest puffed out. "Me? I'm a gangster."

Then, in the one worst thing to happen to big city life maybe ever, drugs came in and did so much harm that they even ruined crime. I had a few years of unmixed joy writing about gangsters who were called Underworld Geniuses and who, when asked to count to anything over ten, bent down and took off a shoe and used toes. Then drugs became the sole business of organized crime. There was no longer any way that I could make a comic figure out of Kid Sally of South Brooklyn, because Kid Sally now sold heroin to schoolkids. Nor would I touch these fables about good gangsters trying to stop bad gangsters from forcing them into the heroin trade. That was what the *Godfather* movie was about. Forcing Carmen Galante to make a half million dollars on heroin. Really. "I will not touch oil," John D. Rockefeller Sr. vowed.

Oh, I sure knew the drugs were coming.

On my first day in Vietnam, in the summer of 1965, I was at this field artillery battery in Bien Hoa, outside Saigon. The soldiers were mostly white, with crew cuts. They had on old undershirts and fatigue pants and were smoking big Pall Malls out of a red pack. "Hitters," one of them said. "We got heroin in them. It's the greatest. Here, you want some?" Then back on Queens Boulevard, a subway motorman, holding a package that had been sent by his son, a sergeant in Vietnam, came around one morning to see Shelly Chevlowe, the bail bondsman. The motorman was afraid to open the package. He figured that Shelly was wise in these things. Shelly tore open the corner, and of course it was all white powder. Vic Juliano, the detective, then at the district attorney's office across the street, had a sample tested. He came back with his lips pursed. "You can't get any stronger than this," he said. Shelly and the motorman took the package out to the sewer and dumped it in. A little melodrama that went nowhere. Because when the sergeant came home from Vietnam and found the father had thrown away his stash, his homecoming money, he tried to strangle the father.

That was some war, that war in Vietnam. When it first ended, the country experienced difficulty in having faith in itself. Thirty years later, drugs are a more ominous part of city life than they ever were.

And in my own little life of writing a column, I lost so many street characters to the drug world that the closest thing to vigorous, amusing dialogue came out of hearings about zoning changes.

The magnitude of the loss could be seen each time I looked over that wall of drugs for a few moments. Even when he was in tight, with the whole federal government on him, an old acquaintance, Anthony (Fat Tony) Salerno knew that the crime they were trying him on, being boss of the whole Mafia, was not as bad as boring people. The federals had bugged a table in an espresso shop where the men decided whether they should kill some guy named Joseph the Goat. The tapes of the bugging were being played in court. Defendant Fat Tony wore big yellow headphones as he listened. I sat in the front row and leaned forward to hear the loudspeaker. The tape went for a half hour and not once was Fat Tony's voice on the tape. He looked at me and made a face that said, "Not bad." I nodded.

Suddenly, all other conversation on the tape ceased and here was the key vote on the murder being delivered so clearly, so instantly recognizable, by Fat Tony Salerno: "Hit!"

Slowly, with a sigh, Fat Tony took off the headphones. Ignoring the marshals he walked over to the gate in front of the spectators' rows. He said loudly, "Did you bring the gun for me? I want to shoot this fuckin' guy." He pointed at the prosecutor.

For so long, it was exhilarating to be around such people. For they were a relief from the respectable, who day after day, night after night, commit the felony of boring others. Why were some people at once engaging desperadoes and so many legitimate people so utterly boring? Could it be the fault of consciousness at birth or do you have the free choice to be this way?

And of the two dinners in my life that I can remember, one was at the old Lighthouse in Bay Shore, Long Island. It was right at the ferry slip to famous Fire Island. The co-owner was Herbie Bruckner, who once was a cheap pyromaniac but had developed into a highly successful arsonist who called himself Marvin the Torch. "I build empty lots," he said.

Directly across the street was a restaurant called Gil Clark's, with which Herbie had a major beef. He served Louis Sherry ice cream, which he felt placed an elegance into his place and also read beautiful on the dessert part of his menu. But Gil Clark's, old and established, had been serving it for years exclusively. They complained to the ice cream company which in turn told Herbie that he no longer could sell the brand. As both restaurants were having trouble making it, the ice cream became somewhat of a focal point for all of Herbie's troubles.

And this night, while I was having dinner, Herbie suddenly called out, "That does it! Gil Clark's goes."

Soon, there was the clang of gas cans coming out of a back room.

Then he changed his mind. He waved at his nearly empty restaurant. "I'm busting out this joint instead," he said. He took out an old school notebook, whose pages were filled with reservations for New Year's Eve, a few weeks off. These were the same reservations he showed fire marshals and insurance adjustors after his last restaurant fire, a year before this. The reservation list absolutely proved that he suffered a tremendous financial loss because New Year's was sold out. Now he said, "All right, everybody out." He was clutching his reservations notebook. We got up to leave. "No," he called out. "That effin' Gil Clark is going. Right now. Up. Boom. Swoosh!"

He went back and forth a couple of times. Finally, he put gas cans on the bar and that cleared the place out. We all were some distance away when Herbie raced up, giggling. At which point, the front wall of his restaurant blew out into the bay. Herbie likes effects. Herbie didn't give the town fire department a chance to get a low moan out of their fire department whistle. The rest of the place was in flames all at once. This was what he called an Apache Indian job. Only a brick chimney and a few smoking timbers remaining.

Drugs ended most stories about arson worth telling. Any characters who played with matches went for real money. Why burn down a restaurant when you can make a fortune for a lifetime selling drugs in a month?

Then computers took the verve out of the whole newsroom and the charm out of the stories. The words on the reporter's screen now were so neat that there could be nothing wrong. The margins, left and right, always perfect, were inhuman. But everybody loved it; it looked great. Send it in. The copy happened to be as boring as it was neat. The reporters all have at least one degree from a good college and can speak at least one other language, but they have been brought up on television and they stare at the computer terminal with the passivity of someone watching a situation comedy. The verbs become so passive that the sentences seem to stop for a commercial. Somewhere, the reporters learn to start a paragraph with sentences that say nothing. They put everything that they can think of into the last sentence of the paragraph. It reads as if they are afraid that the computer will choke them off at the bottom of the screen and, seeing this, they suddenly have to rush everything they know into one sentence. One day, my friend John Kifner of the *Times* newspaper, who had bad hands from repetitive motion on the computer and was doing editing for a while, came out of the place at day's end and winced. "They should close up all the colleges."

Newspaper managements love the new fashion of news reporters, however, because they cause no trouble. They go to some exercise place at lunch and after work they go right home to dinner. It is so much better for marriages, and calmness at work. Their children might be the first generation in a news family to have a somewhat normal life.

And since words for a newspaper come from nervous energy and not propriety, the readers get robbed and the news reporters never live.

Once, when there were newspaper bars, there always was somebody with a real memory who could tell anecdotes that make you smell the people and the room they are in. As you listen the curiosity rises.

Which is the missing emotion. The computer can search files and the LEXIS and NEXIS and find names and facts from everywhere. But anybody who relies solely on just pecking away at little keys to find out what happened is a complete imbecile. How can you be even half alive and not want to go out and see something, talk to somebody, hold a book or papers in your hands and finish what you need and then turn the page, turn it for no reason, learning on the whim, and come upon something so much more delightful and important than anything you first wanted? I would not pay ten dollars to any lawyer who does not go into a library and hold the book in his own hands and begin to read it, look around, come by chance on something he might use. Knowledge by wandering around.

You take these emotions, curiosity, whim, wandering around, out of a day's work and you have a corporation of zombies giving you an array of facts and details not worth space in a wastebasket.

We had a place behind the *Daily News* newspaper, the Gatti Restaurant, with a big bar, where one night, Z. Terzi, the PLO delegate to the United Nations, delivered a political lecture while a crowd of young reporters, many of whom might have been Jewish and were reluctant even to talk to the man, listened. Terzi had negotiated secretly with the United States representative, Andrew Young. The Israeli ambassador, Blum, had started a furor that ended only when Young was out of a job at 4:00 P.M. "A very bad thing happened today," Terzi said. "An ambassador has lost his job. It is one thing to represent interests and defame each other and your countries and races. You may say horrible things, but you are not supposed to lose a job. That is why today a tragedy took place. If Ambassador Young can lose his job, then I, Terzi, can lose my job. I live on East 40th Street. I like it much better than Beirut. I also can tell you that Ambassador Blum is very concerned over this. He had no idea it would go this far. For if Ambassador Young can lose his job, then Ambassador Blum also can lose his job. Ambassador Blum also lives here on the East Side of Manhattan. He does not want to go back to Jerusalem. The first rule of politics everywhere is that nobody should lose a job."

This was the best political talk I have heard in my time in my business and it is nowhere to be found in any file on a computer.

In Costello's, on East 44th Street, a filthy bar with walls that smelled of smoke and were covered with cartoons drawn by James Thurber in order to pay his bills, we had Jim Kahn, who had spent a million days on newspapers, starting with the *Evening Sun*, which ran the "Yes, Virginia" editorial. "Francis Pharcellus Church!" Kahn would announce. That was the name of the *Sun* editorial writer who wrote the piece that would last forever.

"But we were able to balance our brilliance quite nicely," Kahn said. He then would introduce the thieves he had worked with.

"Ed Van Every, who wrote about boxing, charged two dollars a mention for a fighter in training. He used to drop the names in anywhere in the story. When he finished, he read over the copy carefully. He didn't look for mistakes. He just added up the money from the mentions. Every other sentence he made two dollars."

The way I had it is all gone now. The

bars are gone, the drinkers gone. There remain the smartest, healthiest newspeople in the history of the business. And they are so boring that they kill the business right in front of you. A central reason why newspaper circulation is dropping so alarmingly is that reporters have all the excitement of a Formica table.

The newspaper city room, then, has become the home of the boring and homely and stammerers who write in precise terms of how politicians are having difficulty in reaching voters by television. Men without funds for a new car write learnedly about the price of gold. All cannot wait for something to occur that is so trivial that it can be written without thought and the public will be expected to love the story for days, which they do not.

Once, this sort of life was regarded as a form of diphtheria.

With television, you simply follow the money. The people who actually put the news together sit in offices and go nowhere and talk to people almost always only on the phone, and receive the pay of a person spreading asphalt. Then in the middle of the news show, here is the town oddity, the giggling weather man. He gets $600,000 a year. So it is essentially a business for tap dancers. And what I did on Sunday night, back in the apartment in New York, I didn't watch the news because at this point, it had to be important for me to want to watch it, and I knew there would be no such thing.

The suitcases were packed, the plane tickets on a night table. When I was going to bed I was as calm as the room air. My eyes were almost shut when I became so surprised by this absence of fear that I did not trust one moment. Was this feeling of safety something that wasn't really there but was instead just a sign of total numbness?

From the moment this thing started, from the technician taking the angiogram pictures telling me that I officially had an aneurysm, right to now, when I am at the knife's edge, I had not experienced a moment of fear. I had not taken one short breath in fear or stopped what I was doing and become motionless with dread. It was the gift of Grace. Oh, don't tell me it is not there because I will show you that it is. If I had been asked at the start of all this to ask for one thing above all, and it could be granted, the last thing I would have thought of was being allowed to go through these hours without the least bit of fear. At this moment, I was supposed to have a white sheet for a face and instead I was facing a brain operation as if it were a news interview.

This was the first time in my life I was touched so openly by Grace, and that is exactly what it was. All my life I have not liked that hymn "Amazing Grace" because I thought it was some southern Protestant song. Baptists wailing in some country church. It turns out they were singing about something that actually exists; it sure did save a wretch like me. Grace is that instant that comes to ensure that torment shall not prevail. Grace appears when you don't expect it and have asked for nothing. It comes out of the mists to help people at their work. The Catechism for my Catholic Church says that Grace comes to those who teach, who in their teaching exhort and contribute in liberality. I was taught that once, and that is all I had to be told, too. If you do something like write a newspaper column, your liberality is a virtual order to take these immensely unpopular stands on behalf of the poor, the least of us. While doing this, I often saw myself as a great hero, clinging defiantly to a rope across a slippery deck — no, change that to actually standing right up in the bows on watch at night, braving a great storm.

But it takes absolutely nothing to go against public opinion because public opinion is wrong to hold and insane to herald because it is made of a choir of crickets. The sameness of the sound tells you the amount of thought. Nobody stops to realize that something can happen five minutes from now and everybody instantly will think differently. For anybody who writes, the popular fancy is nothing more than a cheap disease. Going against it on the question of race, the single solitary subject that is the arsenic of the soul, can bring rewards in ways that you never were smart enough to ask for.

All those days and nights going to black neighborhoods when you could have passed them up and gone to someplace comfortable.

They are saving me, I told myself.

I could have been someplace nice, and not getting a story from some guy with a handicap trying to sell me crutches. Don't worry about me. I have the instincts needed to always seek comfort. You can't do much about the sins you committed, but it is the things you don't do, the Sins of Omission, that kill. But I speak ex cathedra that you destroy and demolish every thing you've ever done by not recognizing the people living in slavery today because of the color of their skin, and that this slavery is living dead broke from morning to night every day of their lives, and by the design of practically everybody else.

This was the first time in my life that I had been touched so openly by Grace. Yet I still needed something, a tremble, a tremor, a sudden tightening of the windpipe to indicate that this matter is more than somewhat important. How dare there be no tension if a great frightening event was happening to me!

In the sky outside our windows on Sunday night, all of lower Manhattan is silent. The Hudson is dark and difficult to make out. The little lights of Jersey show on the far side. From high over the buildings, with lights blinking and with these beating sounds, came helicopters, one of them dropping to the 30th Street heliport. I could see Abigail Trenk, who runs the heliport. She sits and reads the personal ads in *New York* magazine. Living in the small type somewhere is a real live man. Her dog is outside in the car. She can't bring him in because he is so crazy that he would bite any new boyfriend if one ever came true.

The next thing I see is the trip I took with the Beatles to the Wall Street heliport. This started at Kennedy Airport with these crowds flying down hallways after the

Beatles, who were just off a flight from London. A hand came out of the melee and took my arm. It was Harvey Greenberg, who used to take the boxing photos for Madison Square Garden. He was doing the Beatles' photos. He took me by the arm and I followed him through this mob and out a door and down a flight and out to a helicopter. The Beatles were on it with a couple of managers or whatever and we were all off to Manhattan.

High over Queens, George Harrison decided that sitting strapped into a seat was all too boring and he let out a scream: "We're going down!"

He threw off his seatbelt and began to jump up and down onto the metal floor. "I tell you, we're crashing!"

"Crashing!" Paul McCartney said. He began to jump, too.

Soon, the helicopter was way over the East River and here in the cabin the four Beatles were jumping up and screaming that we were going to crash. The pilots decided to rock the helicopter from one side to the other.

"Down! Down! Down!" McCartney yelled.

When the helicopter landed, they fell on the pilots and kissed them. "You saved us, love!" John Lennon said.

Remembering this just before I fell asleep, I rolled out of bed and started pounding my feet on the floor. I yelled at my wife, Ronnie, "I'm going to die. I'm going to come out of this with my mouth frothing in a wheelchair. I'm going to die. Die, die, die."

Then I fell into bed and passed out.

There was only one light on Broadway when I woke up on the day we were going to Phoenix. "A broken head for every light on Broadway," I announced. I looked out to the right, the building on the block that was nearest the river. It was completely dark all the while I made coffee. Then one light finally appeared. Betty Comden lives there but it couldn't have been her at this hour. The silence of the dark buildings and deserted streets was so heavy that you could hold it in your hands. Nobody in the buildings around me was awake and there was not a light showing on the East Side. Roberts was asleep dreaming about himself. Finally, on my right, a light in the living room of a large apartment went on. Some stock and bond thief who can't sleep for all that he steals. No, let's be nice. A lawyer worrying about a case. Then over at Lincoln Center, the lights on one floor of the white building housing Juilliard students went on.

It was the gymnasium. There, at this hour, what was it, 5:30? a male form appeared on the lighted floor and you could see him taking a shot at a basket. It is a pleasure to look down there on winter evenings and see a crowd of young music students racing about. Good exercise. But if anybody was up shooting baskets at 5:30, then there was a certain confusion about his life. The kid has no idea of who he is. Anthony Mason is out at 5:30 A.M. shooting. He is out there with his navy blue sweat pants with white lettering on both knees. "White Men Can't Jump." This kid at Juilliard, whoever he was, he was about five-seven and 125 pounds, which is a full foot and 150 pounds smaller than Mason and he should have been off in a rehearsal room. I gave a call to Juilliard.

"Security."

"You bet security. You got a fruitcake in your gym. You better get up there with a net for this little psycho. He's supposed to be playing a horn and he thinks he's Anthony Mason."

I watched the gym but I couldn't tell if the security man came there or not. After a while the kid stopped playing with a basketball and the light went off.

I stood on the terrace and stared at the

dark city. Then when my wife got up, she was on the phone about Thanksgiving. No, we won't be here, she was saying. "Well, ah, Jimmy has to have an operation." I saw her looking at me as she talked.

I went over the money in my head. The apartment had been half mine on paper. If I ever came out of this operation and looked at the desert sun and called it a big snow-storm, and wound up at a window of some Arizona nursing home with a strong heart and low blood pressure and for the next twenty-three years pointed out polar bears in the sun, they would have ten liens on the apartment to pay the bills.

I asked Paul O'Dwyer, our lawyer, to put the apartment in Ronnie's name and thus out of reach of a nursing home. Was it dishonest? I don't know. Perhaps it was cunning larceny or shameless evasion of the law. But the guilt crumbled and dissolved as I thought of a life of work being disintegrated by a disease that comes out of a sky and threatens to destroy every hour of work I've ever done.

I'm worried about a roof, not money.

That morning, Burton Roberts was on the phone. "Hello, pal. How are you?"

"I'm nervous. You know I go today for my br—"

"— Can you imagine? Listen to this, will you? It shows you. I don't even have all the families together on the Happy Land settlement yet. I've got that all day."

"I'm nervous. I go for a brain operation today."

"What?"

"Brain operation."

"I didn't know that. Why didn't you tell me?"

"I did."

"No, you didn't. Besides you're not having a brain operation. I can hear you lying right over the phone. Do you know something? Would you believe this? My chin still bothers me from that procedure. You have no idea what a pain in the keester this is. Anyway, how are you, pal?"

"Well, I got this brain oper—"

"— Will you hold on? I got the other phone. Must be Lew Rudin."

He got off the phone and suddenly he came back on. "I got Lew on the other phone."

"So?"

"Lew Rudin!"

Lew Rudin is his landlord who collects rent, but is also a member at rich country clubs.

"What are you going to do, play golf today?" I say with some sarcasm.

"That was yesterday. Let me get back to you."

Later, my daughter Rosemary was downstairs in a cab. Ronnie Eldridge wore a brown and black checked jacket and black pants, and I had on a slate gray suit. The doorman had to come up to get the luggage. I couldn't dare lift anything. I got in the car on the street side and Ronnie on the sidewalk side. My daughter was in the middle. We went up Broadway, where the early rush hour was starting in the small, graceful low old cement building with gabled roof, which was the entrance to the 72nd Street subway station. It is probably the most crowded subway stop in the city, and thus the nation.

At this part of the day, five million people were on their way to work. Into the city they came, from Lawrence and Locust Valley, Rowayton and Ridgefield, Patchogue and Plainview, Danbury and Darien, Freeport and Floral Park, Commack and Cedarhurst, Harmon and Harrison, Greenlawn and Garden City, all those towns that live on the foothills of a city that supports them. They are in resentment and fear and in a social zone separate from the city that supports them.

They drive from Long Island in suburban

insolence, one person to a car that will help clot the city streets, and on trains that break out of trees and into the flat paved miles of two-story semi-attached Queens, into Jamaica Station, which sits disheveled and two flights above the first streets where blacks live. Then the trains rush past the leaves of Forest Hills and run under the river to Penn Station.

From Westchester and Connecticut come other invaders, traveling roads that run beside grass and trees that end with the first desolate towers of the Bronx. Or they come by trains that cause the air to hum as they rush along the trestle over Park Avenue, where it is part of Harlem, the train windows white with newspapers to blot out the broken windows below of those already defeated, the streets of litter and burned cars and the corner bodegas, with children buying anything sweet for breakfast. Running along Park Avenue and never noticing the majestic people still trying to survive in an environment arranged to make survival impossible. The odds they face only can be assailed by spirits that will not cease. On 129th Street, Ned O'Gorman sits on the stoop of his small free private school. Latin is a compulsory subject. "We have a rigorous interior life," he was saying. "I love

Virgil. Why shouldn't a student from Harlem read Virgil?"

Running along the metal trestle over Park Avenue and past the public school for unwed mothers. Kimberley Robinson, sixteen and pregnant, wrote poems at her desk that took her to an East Village reading and a great chance. The train rushes right under the street and into Grand Central Station.

At this hour, all living depends on Manhattan. Car tops glare in the sun on the six bridges over the two rivers. They creep up from the tunnels. Coming from all the subway stops, up the stairs and onto the streets, three million subway riders begin their day. From the East Side they came, from the sedate rich Madison Avenue and Park Avenue buildings. From uptown they came, these short Puerto Ricans and Dominicans walking to stations like Brook Avenue and 138th Street, the ties jammed high up on their shirts, in order for you to see that they have respect, that they wear ties to work, and they strut so proudly to the subway. I go to my *yob*.

And all these millions are thrown working together in a heaving, exciting, jammed, glorious place called New York.

Now the cab went up Amsterdam Avenue, past the old three- and four- and five- story brownstones, with restaurants and shops in the street level. The porters were hosing the sidewalks in front of the unopened stores and restaurants. Up ahead, on the right, was the corner of 93rd and Amsterdam. I don't know whether Ronnie looked up the street. She had lived in a brownstone they had rehabbed during her first marriage.

At 116th Street we went by the red brick buildings, with green copper roofs, of Columbia University. You look down a slope to 125th Street and it is a thousand miles away. And the life I lived stepped out to meet us.

Lawson strides up the corner. Tall, bald, voice booming. There are sounds of rioting everywhere else and on the corner, in a circle of television lights, stands nobody. This was the summer of 1964 and at this time the television stations sent no reporters out to a thing like this. They let the cameramen field the story without direction. So they stood there and pointed a camera at virtually anything and Jim Lawson pushed out of a circle, voice booming. "Harlem civil rights leader," he said.

They put the lights and cameras on him. "I have one message for all the people," he said. Now his teeth bared. "We goin' KILL you!" He never talked like this in his life, but the moment was so unrestricted, and demanded an old movie scene of threatening natives, that Lawson could not restrain himself. The matter on the streets was supposed to be a riot, but in four days only one person was killed, and that appeared to be the result of a personal disagreement. On the first night of these street disturbances, Bill Whitworth, a reporter then, now the editor of the *Atlantic Monthly*, was calling in details from the phone booth on 125th Street and Seventh Avenue. He was the only white in sight and the people in the crowd were calling to him, "Hey, Whitey, are you crazy?" But nothing else.

After delivering his message, Lawson spun and went back to this restaurant on 125th Street, Frank's, where the annual summer meeting of the Harlem numbers bankers was taking place.

I am at the bar with three older women and Horse Steele, a numbers banker, and Lawson asks, "What time is it?"

"Five twenty-five," somebody calls out.

"Good. Put on Channel Seven. They said I'd be on five thirty."

Now the news show comes on and here is Lawson on the small screen, teeth bared like a guard dog. "KILL." A woman ran up the bar and hit Lawson with her purse. "Kill a *fly*."

Ellsworth (Bumpy) Johnson grabbed Lawson by the tie and made the knot run up until it started to choke him and then Bumpy didn't stop until Lawson's eyes rolled and he really was going to be killed.

It was great in the bar. Out in the neighborhoods where whites lived they froze at the sound of the word *kill*. And it was just another perceived threat in a city sky that seemed full of them, and they started moving as no group of people ever moved from a city.

Now the cab went down 125th Street with the sidewalks empty in the hours before the street peddlers filled them. On the right was the dusty five-story building with the sign saying "Blumstein's." Once, it was a department store and now it is dead. It was here in 1958 that a hysterical woman stabbed Martin Luther King Jr. with a brass letter opener as he was autographing books. The first to rush in were two police officers, Al Howard and Phil Romano.

A woman from the mayor's office, Anne Hedgman, screamed, "Take it out." She reached for the opener.

Phil Romano told himself, "If she touches it, he's dead." His hand flashed out and locked on Anne Hedgman's hand.

Staring at the letter opener in King's chest, Romano said, "God forbid a sneeze. God forbid a cough."

Al Howard looked Martin Luther King in the eyes and said, "Don't move and don't breathe. Can you do that for me? Don't move and don't breathe."

Out on the street, the rumor spread that King had been murdered. Thousands showed up. Let one hand go out to comfort King and jar the letter opener, and he was a dead man. Howard told the crowd to form two lines and leave an alley and they would see Dr. King brought out alive onto 125th Street. Then he was waving to an ambulance, walking back and forth with an official swagger. Inside the store, Romano and a couple of others carried King out the back door and to an ambulance on an empty street. Then Romano and Howard went to the hospital and stood guard at the operating room doors as doctors cut the opener out of King.

Riding in this cab, I can see King right now. It was in the moments before his march on Washington started and he seemed the least bit nervous. By now, he knew he had more to worry about than a letter opener. Only a few feet away, high school students from Danville, Virginia, were lined up and clapping their hands and stamping their feet in the sun. They wore brown overseas caps with "Danville" in gold lettering, and blinding white shirts and brown ties and brown skirts or pants. Then they snap-turned to the left and faced King, feet stamping, their eyes gleaming, their faces so filled with joy and hope that all these people standing with cameras and notebooks had tears in their eyes. Everybody who saw them said, "There goes Danville." For at this time, 1963, the South and Danville in particular still kept its Tobacco Road customs. These were the same school kids who only a few weeks before had been dragged out of a lunch counter and were battered and beaten bloody and were going to be kept in jail for more beatings for a long time. Then lawyers William Kunstler and Arthur Kinoy, down from New York, went into court. Kinoy, who was five-two and weighed 95 pounds, had looked up a federal statute from the Reconstruction era that gave freed slaves the right to take a local case into federal court right away. The local judge in Danville was named Mackie. While his family published all the law books for the state of Virginia, he appeared to have trouble reading. He said he could find no statute. Then Kinoy got up on the bench and placed a finger on the statute and ran his finger along and then said aloud for the judge, "Now right here it says that you must allow the cases to go to federal district court and you must allow bail." The judge followed the old law and the blacks were released, all the Danville kids walked out of court with their legs intact. Now they were stamping and clapping in front of Martin Luther King.

I had a thousand drinks in Queens the night before this and I was looking for water when all of a sudden the street moved and I was carried along by people clapping and singing on their way to the Lincoln Memorial. I walked with Bayard Rustin and A. Philip Randolph and Walter Reuther. They talked about the only political word worth mentioning, *jobs*. We got to the Lincoln Memorial and I had this fierce hangover thirst. I went to the one water fountain in the rotunda, but it was broken. I tried to get into the men's room, but a priest was standing in front of it and wouldn't let me pass. He said the archbishop was inside with John Lewis of Atlanta, then with a black youth organization. They were arguing about part of Lewis's speech that they said was totally inflammatory. Today, it would be so tame that nobody would bother to say it, but on this day in 1963, it raised the Catholic fear of blacks, and that never does take much. If Lewis didn't remove the passages from his speech, the priest told me, the archbishop was going to take all Catholic support from the march and go home.

"I'm a Catholic," I said. "I'm not going anywhere. I'm thirsty. Give me something to drink."

He would not move. I saw marshals starting to block off the seats on the steps so I had to go out and find a seat for myself on the marble steps. I stared out at the long reflecting pool, with sun sprays on the water, and got thirstier. The crowd sat along the edges of the pool, way down to the end, with those at the edge of the pool sticking bare feet into the water. Mahalia Jackson got up and sang. Thousands of feet kicked in the reflecting pool in time to her singing. They raised all these little geysers of white water; the sun shone and my throat closed.

By the time Martin Luther King got up, I was distracted by thirst. I heard the speech, all right. He was speaking about five yards away. "I have a dream. . . ." He lifted everybody onto a green plateau at the top of the highest mountain in the history of all people. The greatness of his speech had difficulty in coming through my parched discomfort.

When he was finished, I rushed up the steps and into the men's room. I put my mouth to the faucet like a tanker being re-fueled. At the newspaper's bureau in the National Press Building, I sat in the late afternoon and heard the rush of birds out-side and listened to everybody in the office talking in awe of King's speech. The one I guessed had been all right.

Well, I knew what to do. I sat at the typewriter and thought about the Danville kids and made myself emotional and had my eyes filled with tears as I started writing about the greatness of the day.

In all the years since, whenever they show King's "I have a dream" speech, I call out in my house, "I was there. See on the steps? I was right there. History. I remember that all my life."

Al Howard, the police officer who helped King through the stabbing, was a profes-sional and he got up every day and was ready to do it for somebody else. Still, he became bitter after King's assassination in Memphis. Now just the other night at the bar he now owns, Showman's, only a block away from the closed Blumstein department store, he says, "I guess I got him ten more years but they killed him anyway."

As the cab was passing Blumstein's, I was telling this story about King's march for the twentieth time and my wife, having heard it from Al Howard himself, asked if I ever saw the other cop, Phil Romano.

Yes, I did. I saw Romano after one of Martin Luther King's birthdays. He was still on the job, at the same precinct, the 28th, and he had a community precinct council meeting to attend, and on the way to the meeting, he parked his car behind Blumstein's and sat alone and listened as the radio played parts of the "I have a dream" speech. I saw him later that day and he told me, "I turned to ice. I'm not ashamed to say I cried. I cried the night he was killed. I cried today. I'm not ashamed of it."

Past Blumstein's, the cab was across the Triborough Bridge and when the parkway traffic to the airport backed up, the cab swung up the hill and onto Queens Boulevard and here was so much of the history of my life in my city.

Here is Klein the Lawyer in his white Lincoln going down Queens Boulevard. Somebody drives. Klein comes through the open roof with both arms up and he is waving to people on the street. "Thank you!" he yells. Now the driver hands up a car phone. Klein says into the phone, "Where am I? Heaven."

He is a short man who always was running across the wide boulevard from his office in the Silver Towers to the criminal court. One hand clutched his hair to keep it from blowing away. He had thick glasses and a potbelly. He wore high heels to give him some height. He was so sure that he was irresistible that he took a thousand dance lessons so he would be the best dancer on Queens Boulevard. Once, he won two straight murder cases with the same defendant. He took to the dance floor at the Part One bar and spun like a top, shaking a tambourine. Suddenly, he was hit with an attack of narcolepsy. He sat down at a table of strangers with his eyes shut. His head hit the table. One woman screamed. She covered her face and waited for an ambulance. Nobody in the bar who knew Klein would think of calling an ambulance. The woman heard a tambourine shaking. She looked up. Right over her head. Klein was up dancing.

Klein held all his meetings on the traffic island in the middle of Queens Boulevard on the theory that they could not bug the place. It was here that Klein decided to have all clients use the Queens County defense:

"How could I commit a crime? I live in a house."

I marveled at Klein's record. Klein's footprints ran from this traffic island through the entire city and all the way to the top of the nation's political turmoil. Klein became national in 1982 when his client Morris Alpert burned down a store that was losing money in Queens. Twenty-one firemen were injured. Klein brought up a plea bargain to the assistant district attorney, Geraldine Ferraro Zaccaro. She only could hear firemen chanting her name when she won a conviction at a big trial. "She is going to run for Congress and then try president," Klein reported to Morris.

"What does that make me?" Morris said.

"Part of her dream."

After Morris was convicted, Klein the Lawyer gave most enthusiastic interviews about Ms. Ferraro's ability as a prosecutor. The night before Geraldine was nominated at the Democratic National Convention in San Francisco in 1984, I sat next to her husband in the suite and said, "Are we all right here?"

And he said, "Listen, we've had six years to get ready for this." I didn't realize he was talking about the statute of limitations. And then as it must happen in Queens, immediately after the convention, all these blue suits from the Republican National Committee were in the basement file room of the Queens Civil Court clamoring for files on old civil cases that involved husband John Zaccaro and were not in proper order. That means the money was short. And out on Queens Boulevard, with crowds churning on the boulevard, here was Klein the Lawyer announcing, "Why didn't they give me the guardianships? I can use somebody else's money just like Johnny Zaccaro."

On a Sunday, I married Ronnie Eldridge and left Queens Boulevard to live in Manhattan. The very next day, Klein was standing in front of the Pastrami King with an arm draped over a parking meter. "Look at this! It doesn't even look like an oil well, either."

Klein and three others made up a company that collected overtime parking fines. They would collect the fines, and then keep them. Of course people would pay. "We will let a leopard into their house," Klein said.

One partner, Donald Manes, got the city to give them collections work. This was because he had an elected job called Queens borough president. The only responsibility was not to get caught. He even shirked that.

One partner, my friend Shelly Chevlowe,

died and I was in Schwartz's Funeral Home, Queens Boulevard, giving the eulogy. Klein is in the front row, in tears. So is Donald Manes.

Out on the sidewalk, fat Geoff Lindenauer, from the city's Parking Violations Bureau, is telling a lawyer from another collection company, "Donald says that from now on, you pay me. I'm supposed to get the money and bring it to him."

They steal while I cry.

At which point it fell apart. The FBI went up to one of the partners and said, "Could we talk to you?"

"About what?"

"About parked cars in the City of New York."

"Sure," the partner said. "Could I make one phone call first?"

He dialed Klein the Lawyer.

Immediately after that, Klein stood in the traffic island on Queens Boulevard and watched a bus rushing toward him. He thought of jumping in front of it. "Let Donald Manes jump." He stepped back. Manes did not jump. He tried suicide with a knife. He wound up in a hospital. I went there and heard a nurse fighting with two men over a parking space. They showed her FBI identification. I ran right to Klein on Queens

Boulevard. He said, "Stay away from here. It is very dangerous. Can't you see that the boulevard just blew up?"

When our *Daily News* newspaper came out with a story about civic virtue on Queens Boulevard, Manes went into the kitchen drawer for a carving knife and he stood there and plunged it into his chest. Doctors, when giving themselves a needle for anything, usually miss out of terror the first couple of times. Manes did it with a large knife in one. He did not hesitate. He went right for his heart with this knife. With a terrible strength he plunged into his chest, deep in, right through the sheath of muscle and gristle and between the rib bones and, in one chance out of a thousand, right into the heart.

When they called me at home and told that Manes was gone, I went right to bed. It was maybe the one time in life that a news story knocked me down right away. I do not remember much of anything about the day, which I spent in bed.

The game for Klein was to get to the United States attorney's office and cry extortion before they came around with handcuffs and said, "Bribe." It is nothing more complicated than blaming the other guy for extortion before he reports to authorities

271

that you bribed him. The first man in usually remains out of prison. But all action must be blindingly fast at this point.

"I want to wait and see what happens," Klein said.

He waited all right. He waited in the federal joint in Panama City, Florida.

Whenever I saw one of these government scandals start coming out in a newspaper, there is granular motion, with one new fact pressing down on another, causing a tumbling motion that causes something that nobody ever dreamed about to be hurled out in the open. People who thought they were hidden forever in an unseen life suddenly are alone in a light, with a tumult around them. Just the mere act of typing at one desk in a city room starts motion somewhere else. So while the stories being typed were about Manes and extortion, and with Klein still only in the eighth or ninth paragraphs, on the other side of the city room, a woman reporter suddenly had an unsigned letter saying that the Bronx Democratic leader was involved with the parking ticket collections. This was the sort of letter usually considered to be "crank mail." But in time of scandal even letters in crayon suddenly turn true. That put it in another borough of the city. Then she found that the same people in the parking scandal were looting a Bronx defense plant. The owner was a man named John Marriotta, who was such an Hispanic favorite with Ronald Reagan that he had been brought in to address a cabinet session. He could not read or write so he didn't understand any of the issues. But he did say, "God Bless America!" And Reagan beamed.

Now the stories, separate at first, began to merge and you found Manes's name everywhere and Klein the Lawyer moved up to the third paragraph in both cases. Then it went national. Two congressmen, Mario Biaggi and Robert Garcia, were indicted for stealing from the defense plant. And then they busted Garcia's wife, and when they were convicted and sentenced, they became the first mom-and-pop convicts in the history of American politics. Then into court and cells went three city commissioners, a Bronx borough president, the Bronx County Democratic leader, and two National Guard generals. One of them, Boom Boom Castellano, always wore his general's uniform to impress purchasing agents. He was selling an automatic parking meter. Castellano used to stand in front of a mirror and salute himself. Oh, yes, this thing got going good.

But these are stories about cheap little

local politicians and whether they live or are squashed like beetles on a jailhouse floor is unimportant. What matters is that whenever there is stealing by politicians the money or the betrayal of public trust is unimportant, but the distractions caused by thievery destroy the government that is supposed to protect you. So in New York City at the time all this was going on, there was a mayor named Koch who sat in the center of the largest scandal in city history and said he knew nothing about it. He was, he said, the only honest man in City Hall. And while he preened and denied, there were 18,106 citizens of his city murdered, almost two thousand a year, every year, three quarters of them by guns, and he noticed nothing.

By 7:00 A.M. we were at the gate for the plane to Phoenix.

I thought about my son Christopher. I could see him sitting in his first-grade classroom, off in the last seat, his head low so perhaps nobody would see him. There was something on the blackboard, and he alone in the room didn't have the breath of an idea what it was. When the others read aloud from a book, he memorized one page of what they said aloud and then at home he held the book and recited the page for his mother. When she showed him another page, he didn't know a word of it. His mother got a woman who taught special education students to look in on the class. She told us to get him out of the school right there, that he sits like a dog. He needs a lot of testing. That took six months to find out exactly what it was. My wife did most of it. I went with her as much as possible. I wound up in the office of a doctor who said he had a screening test for the ear, which he said was the cause of dyslexia. Then I went to a school parent-teacher's fair at a Catholic grammar school and I can't remember which one it was, I was at so many, but the nun in charge had me looking into a box that simulated dyslexic sight. A word I was looking at went crazy, shooting off to the top and bottom, and had me baffled.

Then Rosemary was taking him to neurologists and I didn't like the word to begin with. What were they trying to tell me, that he's retarded or crazy?

"He just sees things mixed up," his mother said. "We have to find a place where he can learn."

She taught him to write by first writing something in light pencil and then having him use a pen to write over it. That went on for a couple of years. He had no idea of right or left until he cut his left hand and needed stitches. He could refer to the scar when he had to know left from right. He went through seven grammar schools. When he would try to read for too long, he became dizzy. By visiting so many schools and talking to teachers, we learned that there was a circle of reading teachers for students with dyslexia. We had to go through somebody at Harvard, who recommended us to a woman named Katrina De Hirsch on the East Side of Manhattan. I remember going to the newsstand on her corner and picking up *Time* magazine, which had a review saying my book about Watergate, *How the Good Guys Finally Won*, was the best political book of the year. I folded it in half and walked into her brownstone office like I was a college dean. She immediately humiliated me and made it sound as if I had started all my son's troubles. She sent us to a woman in Washington Heights, Ruth Molleson. Somebody said she was Henry Kissinger's sister. Rosemary had to drive the kid up there, sit outside in the car and wait, then drive him home.

Through so much of this, his mother was ill. The most important step Christopher ever took was when we decided to put him into the regular grammar school, P.S. 101

in Forest Hills, in the sixth grade. After these years of being in a "special school" he was elated to be like everybody else. His work improved so quickly it was hard to realize that it was happening. He spent so long adjusting to the riddle and he was just starting to solve the flying words on the page. At least some of the problem became mine. He worried about every bump and even faint bruise on his face that I used to berate him for worrying so much, all the time forgetting that people with dyslexia are always overly concerned with their faces. Don't ask me why. And for sure, don't ask me how he outgrew it.

He went to three high schools. He wanted to go to Boston College. He had to go to a junior college first. After that he went to Boston College at night for a year, then transferred to days. It was heartbreaking that his mother was dead on the day he graduated. It was a bright sunny day in the football stadium and his aunt, his mother's sister, looked at him and said, "This is the last one."

So we all sure know that while it took great effort, Christopher's brain outgrew its problem and for that we all have to thank his brain, Christopher first.

Into the bright Phoenix morning we came

on Monday, November 21, 1995. We got to the Arizona Biltmore hotel by 11:30 A.M. and instead of going to the room, which involved too many smiling room clerks and bellmen for me, I went into the coffee shop and had a hamburger made out of turkey. It had no taste. If it isn't fried grease, it isn't good. My wife and daughter came in and had salads while I had coffee. Then we went out into the sun and lawns and took a cab to the hospital. The light brick color of the Barrow Neurological Building rose from a wide empty street, with a larger hospital, St. Joseph's, on the opposite side.

The Barrow driveway was blocked by cars and by these men walking around in form-fitting suits and with ear radios and Secret Service haircuts and sunglasses. We had read somewhere that the Saudi Arabian queen had taken an entire floor of the hospital and had over forty doctors besides the ones here. She had Saudi Arabian 727 planes sitting at the airport.

I was about to snarl that we were spending tax money on these robots to guard a woman nobody ever heard of when I looked at the agents more closely. They had no government behind them, only some local security agency. Plant guards in blue suits. I walked right past them.

There was this one large entrance but on the left was a glass door with Robert Spetzler's name on it. You just went through the doors and into a small waiting room with a counter straight ahead as you entered. Three or four women receptionists sat in a room behind the counter. The waiting room windows looked out on the hospital driveway and a small parking lot and that was it. In an alcove was a soda machine and a pay phone booth.

When one of the women saw me walking in, she looked up and said, "Yes?"

And now it was official.

I walked up to the woman at the desk and she gave me forms for medical insurance. I had no cards. In October, I became sixty-five and at my newspaper office some accountant didn't read my contract with the paper and took me off the medical coverage on the premise I would be covered by Medicare. I never knew anything about it and they never notified my wife or accountant. If anybody did tell me, I never would have done a thing. I don't go to offices where I have to stand on line. And especially not for some Medicare. That was for old busted valises.

When the woman behind the counter found I had no cards or papers or anything to show that they were going to get paid, she frowned.

"Don't worry about it," I told her.

"We need some hospitalization insurance," she said.

"You'll get paid, don't worry about it."

"No, you misunderstand me. I don't want money. All I want is your insurance."

"I don't have any. Send me the bill and we'll send a check."

She nearly choked.

"How much of this can I put on my credit card?" I asked.

Then my wife came up to the counter. She started right in, saying I was wrong, that I did have Medicare coverage that she had taken me to an office herself, although I chose not to remember that. It was just that I didn't have a number yet and besides, there was her policy that now had me as a spouse and another policy called Medigap.

She told me to go and sit down and she resumed explaining to the woman how there actually were three policies or something, I didn't know what it was all about, but when I sat down my life started trying to move across my mind, and I didn't want to see it anymore. How could it be about anything else but me being broke?

It wasn't a long wait on the clock, only

about fifteen minutes, which was just long enough for you to begin to notice that you were waiting. I had been in Phoenix twice before this, the first time in 1963, when there were newspaper awards that were announced during a large reception conducted by Eugene Pulliam, the publisher of the Phoenix *Arizona Republic*. He also owned newspapers in Indianapolis and Huntington, Indiana, the last one standing as a future for his grandson, Dan Quayle. One of the people in charge of the night was Clare Boothe Luce and she had Theodore H. White down from New York with her. He wrote *The Making of the President 1960*. She had White wearing a pith hat and if she took a step he followed. At a party in Pulliam's house in Paradise Valley, I was standing in a white rug that came to my ankles and Clare Boothe Luce told me that I should quit newspapers and write important books.

"And eat what while I'm writing?" I said.

"Oh, I'm sure there are certain people who could contribute to you as patrons," she said. She looked at Pulliam, who nodded.

And my wife, the former Rosemary Dattolico, now said to Clare Boothe Luce, "He thinks different than you do."

"I'm sure we have differences of opinion, but, ah . . ."

"I think different than you, too," Rosemary said. "I know one thing. If Jimmy wears a hat like that, then he has to come home with a lion."

I have to say that the second wife, Ronnie Eldridge, the one with me now in the hospital, would have reacted precisely the same. So what that proves, once again, is that I know more about the woman you should marry than anybody.

Clare Boothe Luce was the wife of Henry Luce, who owned *Time* magazine and *Life* magazine, which at the time also was supposed to be a strong voice. I saw them again in Honolulu when I was on my way to Vietnam and they talked so learnedly about Vietnam that I kept my mouth shut. Not out of any deference, of which I have none, but because I thought they knew. Oh, they knew. I'll tell you who knew. As the result of the war showed, the Vietnamese knew.

I walked over to get a can of soda but then I decided to just walk out into the hall. I found a large plaque that said Barry Goldwater had donated something to the hospital. A woman in a blue smock sitting at a desk saw me looking. "He was here for a back operation and then he and the nurse got married." I told myself that I would try to look him up when I got out of here. Goldwater started this whole notion of a right wing in America and he did it with an honesty that the politicians who succeeded him cannot tolerate. When they won all these elections, including knocking my friend Cuomo out in New York, not one of them mentioned Goldwater's name.

I saw him make his last speech when he ran for president in 1964. Up at the Utah border, in Fredonia, in the cold dusk, at an airport with one lone bulb over the doorway to the brick terminal hut. High school kids in windbreakers and Levi's were sitting on the roof with their boots dangling in front of the bulb. There was cattle wire on the other side of the one runway and after that, red sandstone hills cloaked with cold dusk. Low cedar trees were dark knots. Straight out, where the hills rose into mountains, the sky was charcoal gray and pink and blue, with jet contrails mixed into it like finger painting. There were eighteen hundred people there, which was a lot for Fredonia. I remember they stood in wind that whipped at the autograph pads in their hands. Goldwater was wonderful. He spoke lovingly of the land and said that he wanted the America in front of him to be the America for everybody. I remember telling myself, "Just don't think of three million in Brooklyn and you'll love this."

Then the next morning, election day, at the Paradise Valley School in Phoenix, Goldwater was on line to vote. Only a couple of us from newspapers were with him. There were no security people ruining the day. The television cameras were not live. This election was in 1964, which is five thousand years away from today, when a candidate like this would arrive with a hundred agents, who either push people or stare at them as if they are murder suspects. But now, Goldwater stands behind his wife, Peggy. She has on a sunback tan dress and Goldwater has a felt tip pen and he is playing tic-tac-toe on her back and she doesn't notice and he smiles. There are no security men around him and maybe there are a few television cameramen by the voting booth. But there was no line of smoked glass cameras, red lights on, smothering any chance for being natural. So the man could just stand there in a shirt and khaki pants. I remember him telling me, "This was all too long. Anything I had to say I could've said in thirty days. Anything Johnson had to say couldn't have taken him all that much longer. This thing is out of hand. The British have the right idea. Say it and get the hell out of the way and let the public tell you what they heard."

His wife went into the voting booth and their son dropped to one knee and took a picture of her legs in the booth. Goldwater smiled. He liked it.

The trouble is, a few weeks before this, Goldwater had been up to the dining room at the *Herald-Tribune* newspaper to have lunch with Jock Whitney, the publisher, and Jim Bellows, the editor, and these other executives and I wedge my way into the room and say nothing and Goldwater says that we have to go right into Vietnam, not stand around and hope like we did in Korea. "We have to invade North Vietnam and go through Hanoi to the Chinese border."

"What if the Chinese come in?" he is asked.

"Then we don't stop. There'll be no Yalu River here. We fight them where they are and bomb them where they live. Peking is the capital. Bomb that."

"But wouldn't that mean Russia comes in? What would happen then?"

"Oh, then we'll have a nuclear war."

Standing here and looking at this plaque I could feel right away the shock that came when he said that. The lesson in modern

American politics did not come until Gold-water lost everywhere in the country to the peace candidate, Lyndon Johnson. When Johnson came back as a stirring life-saving peace victor to the White House after the election, his best assistant, Bill Moyers, found that on Johnson's desk that first morning was a list of targets in North Vietnam to be bombed.

I came back from the hall plaque and into the waiting room and a woman was at the door alongside the desk and called my name. We went inside and followed her a few steps down a hall and she opened a door to a bare small room, only a little bigger than a cubicle. We went in and sat down. My wife and I were on chairs and my daughter sat on a stool. The room had no windows and there were no pictures on the wall. You put your own pictures there as you sat. Imagination puts a painting on the mind. Somebody wrote that. If I can't remember the writer's name, then it's mine.

Out in the world that doesn't count, there were at this moment people sitting in offices a hundred times bigger than this, with paintings on the wall and elaborate phones and computers and faxes and carpet and huge picture windows with a view.

The men in those rooms were trying to

decide if they should print a Spanish word on the yellow Cheerios box.

Here, where the man merely works with opening up heads to the very brain, the room was so small that if he tried to get in with a staff they wouldn't fit.

Now, sitting calmly but without a thought crossing my mind, I waited. And the door opened and Spetzler walked in quickly. It was a small room but he still walked in quickly. That first step into the room told you who he was. Spetzler was dressed for the operating room. A blue cap was tied to his head with a white cord. He was tall and had a neat mustache. Big strong tanned arms came out of a blue short-sleeved shirt. The hands were long and graceful. He was pleasant and his eyes inquired kindly and he was solicitous, but in charge. Don't worry about that.

It was obvious that he wasn't sure what I was, but he knew I had done something to get here this way. All big guys can tell at a look whether the other guy is the least bit successful. It doesn't matter what you have on or where you sit. You wear any good years.

I had read about him. Spetzler is fifty and was born in Würzburg, Germany. His cousin was killed over a bombing plot against Hitler. His father, who had been a watchmaker in Germany, came here with an invention for a quartz clock that he brought to Westclox, a company in Illinois. Spetzler was five when he arrived in La Salle–Peru, Illinois, with his family. He went to one of those good small midwestern colleges, Knox, and said he wanted to be a neurosurgeon and nothing else. He studied at Case Western in Cleveland and later on, when he was passed over as the head of the neurosurgery department, he left. He is not very good at being ignored. He came to Phoenix and built this center in the sun, the Barrow Neurological Institute, which now is a seven-story building attached to St. Joseph's Hospital. On this day he had me and, of much less importance as far as I was concerned, the queen of Saudi Arabia.

What else did I read? Spetzler has a baritone voice and is an old swimmer. He has a large house in Paradise Valley with a lap pool. He did backstroke in college. He does things like ski out of helicopters. He takes chances for sport, and for a living.

In his office, which was right across the hall from this small room, he has a concert piano in a cubicle. He listens to himself play over earphones. He also has a large fish tank and three television monitors that show the operating rooms and what is going on in them.

He came in here with no records with him and was going to do no examining. He said this would be a pretty much straightforward brain operation for an aneurysm. Of which I was sure there was no such thing.

"How long does it take?" my daughter asked.

"Time is meaningless," he said. "The only people who notice that are the ones waiting. When you are operating, you don't notice it."

Until now, I had slid and hid from the one subject I now brought up: "By the way, how do you do the operation?" Spetzler took his finger and ran it across my forehead and down my right temple in front of the ear and stopped even with the start of the ear. He had a nice touch, but he was outlining half my head being taken off.

"We had your case presented by the visitor from New York University," he said. He wasn't sure of the name. He meant David Chalif. It turns out he isn't good at any names. He looked at the assistant, who also didn't know.

"Okay then," he said. "We'll see you in the morning."

Then, just before leaving, he asked,

"What kind of work do you do?"

I was elated. Know my angiogram film; the face and name don't count. But the politician in my wife suddenly flew out of her mouth. "He's a Pulitzer Prize winner!"

Never before this had either of us ever mentioned the award. When Spetzler saw me looking in astonishment at my wife, he said, "No, that is important that you tell us. If you're a writer, we have to take that into consideration. Your skills come from certain parts of the brain. If you did something else for a living, then we would think in another way.

"We operated on a truck driver who had an aneurysm in a place right where all his motor skills come from. We had to be extremely careful of that part of him."

So if I was a moving man and it came to a decision between shoulder mobility and the objective case, I would be pushing a piano and saying "between you and I."

Now he said, "I'll see you tomorrow."

Beyond that, there wasn't much to discuss. I wasn't going anyplace and he'd be around. We would meet in the morning. I said fine and he smiled and nodded and was gone.

We filled in admittance forms out at another desk and were escorted to a bare room with one window looking out on the street. The room was on the fourth floor. When I came in I had on my sports jacket, which I noticed looked like it had been caught in a thousand doors. There were only wire hangers in the closet. I hung up the jacket and a nurse came in and handed me this blue gown with the tie strings. The only time I ever looked at anybody wearing one of these things was in the course of making a living. Otherwise, I spent my whole life turning my head from the gowns because they meant sick and wounded and helpless. They took me for X rays and blood tests. I came back and sat and talked with my wife about the only thing on my mind: that by this time tomorrow I could be the priest who felt nothing. One remark made two weeks ago and it dominated me.

"What if I can't put three words together?" I said.

"Don't be silly."

"Did you send the papers on the house? I signed them all right."

"Yes," she said.

I could not believe it. She was not telling me the truth. The tone in her voice told me that she sure had not sent them. Lie she cannot. In other words, by tomorrow night I could be sitting here unable to react to the sound of my own name and I also could be out of a house. No, it's worse. She could be the one out of a house.

A priest came in and asked if I needed anything and said a prayer aloud and we stood with him. Then I stretched out on the bed and I remember putting my hands under my head in order to philosophize properly. Only I didn't have anything to say deeper than the weather.

James Miller, a doctor in a white coat, came in just as the first dusk was on the street outside the window. He said he wanted to take a few things down. "I'm going to be taking care of you after surgery," he said.

"I'm all right, don't worry about it," I said.

"How long have you had the diabetes?" he said.

"I don't have diabetes. I have like half a case."

"You do not. You have diabetes," my wife said. "Now answer him."

"I just did."

"No, you didn't."

"Didn't I answer you?" I said to Miller.

"No."

I exhaled in defeat.

"I think we ought to give you some insulin before you go in," he said.

"Never! When I had the angiogram in New York they were going to do that. Then he took my count and he didn't have to do anything. You call up the doctor. Andrew Drexler. He'll tell you."

"The stress from surgery can cause the blood sugar to elevate considerably. We'd like to take a little precaution."

"I don't drink," I said. If that didn't answer everything.

"Will you stop being a baby?" my wife said.

"They're going to open my head and my hand doesn't even shake. Look." I held the right hand out. It was steady as a rail. I could not believe that it wasn't vibrating. And so I said triumphantly, "See?"

Miller was unimpressed. What was probably contributing to his persistence was that before the night was over, he had to sign a letter clearing me for surgery, stating that my heart and lungs and diabetes were able to weather any surgery, barring any unexpected results in the tests now in the laboratory.

Miller said he would be back after a while.

I was talking about myself at a rapid length to prove that I was unconcerned. I noticed my wife and daughter hunching up against the shouting. Then a tall man in street clothes came in. He had a mustache and pleasant smile. He introduced himself as Peter Raudzens. He was the neuro-anesthesiologist. "I'll be taking care of you in the morning," he said.

I became attentive. "You can blow the whole game with the anesthesiologist," my friend Charley Peters always said. "They can make a monkey out of you for real." He learned that while he was in Attica; I am not snobbish about the source of knowledge.

Raudzens asked me about my history and said he had read the charts on me and thought I'd do quite well. "We'll give you a little Valium in the morning to relax you, get you a little drowsy and then we'll put you out for a while."

Then he said he was out of Harvard and that he always admired Tip O'Neill.

"Was he really a good guy the way I think he is?" he asked me. "You knew him, didn't you?"

"Do I know him? Let me tell you." I accept all chances to hear my own voice tell a story. O'Neill was from Cambridge, and had replaced Jack Kennedy as congressman. When he became the House majority leader, he pushed for the impeachment of Richard

Nixon. He went on to become speaker. So I say to Raudzens: "I'm in Tip O'Neill's office in the Capitol on the night that Nixon quit on television. O'Neill watches it and when it's over he turns off the television and says, 'Let's eat!' That meant gargle and food. On the way down to Duke Zeibert's, we went past the White House. There was some traffic on Pennsylvania Avenue, with people slowing to look at the White House, with the lights on upstairs. Not heavy traffic. Just some traffic moving slowly. Now a motorcycle cop comes along. He makes a U-turn and parks in front of the White House. The cop gets off and walks into the middle of Pennsylvania Avenue and begins waving the traffic along. We stop across the street by the park and watch. O'Neill has just been one of the big guys moving to get Nixon out. If he had any fears that he hurt the country he doesn't have them now, believe me. Here was the government of the largest country on earth changing hands at night. And all you had was one motorcycle cop. There was not one tank, one platoon of soldiers, one voice bellowing orders; there was no crowd screaming or rushing the gates. Just one police officer, directing traffic. And in the car, Tip O'Neill says, 'Geez. This has to be the damnedest place in the whole world.' It sure was that night."

Raudzens said he'd see me in the morning. He left. Soon, Dr. Miller walked back in.

"I spoke to your endocrinologist in New York," he said, "and he agrees with everything I say."

He was wearing cowboy boots and when I asked him about them he said that he had a cattle feeding business in Colorado with three thousand head.

I perked up.

"How do you kill them?"

"Blow to the head. They shoot a high-speed piston into them."

I cut right in. "And then they pull it right out and use the piston on the next one. I know that. I saw them do it in Derry. That's in Northern Ireland. They had this abattoir and I see them shooting sheep. Skinch McCarthy used to steal sheep hides and bring them home. You should have smelled his house."

When nobody took me up on my conversation, I became silent. Then Miller left.

BRESLIN, JIMMY
00046078150 M
VITAL SIGNS: Pending at this time.

HEENT: Examination reveals lateral gaze at the left eye.

NECK: Supple.

CHEST: Clear.

CARDIAC: Regular rate and rhythm without murmur or gallop.

NEUROLOGICAL: Nonfocal, other than above.

IMPRESSION:

1. History of diet and Glynase-controlled diabetes mellitus. The patient does have fairly good followup for this problem. I suspect control is adequate.

2. Right cerebral aneurysm, presented for surgical intervention.

RECOMMENDATIONS: Barring any significant abnormality on preoperative laboratory, the patient appears to be at low risk for surgery. I see no medical complications at this time. Barring any surprise on baseline laboratory, he is cleared for surgery.

— JAMES A. MILLER, M.D.

My daughter and my wife kissed me good night and said they would see me in the morning. It was eight o'clock. I had about ten hours to go.

I was left to myself, looking out the window at an empty street. A couple of cars passed. No people. No lighted stores. I sat and stared out. I was alone on an empty street. That is exactly what I wanted if anything went wrong.

I hated to bring him up, but I hoped that I had one thing in me from my father. He died in 1974 in a nursing home by the railroad station in Miami. The guy from the *Miami Herald* called me up when it happened. I never told my mother or sister about it, but they were going to put my father into Potter's field until the newspaper called me. The woman who ran the nursing home said he was "a gutter rat, a complete loner. He had a chest pain and we said he should get a doctor, but he refused. He wouldn't talk. He just wanted a cigarette. We had him on filter tips because his circulation was so bad that he didn't feel the regular Chesterfields when they burned right to his fingers." He left two names as his nearest relatives. Mine, and I had neither seen nor spoken to him in over fifty years. The address he had for me was a dead newspaper. He told the nurse that he had tried to talk to me, but I was too busy. He listed his other relative as "Miss Fortune, 28 Ocean Dr., Miami Beach." The address was the Play House Bar, and Miss Fortune was not at that address. I'm sorry he wrote that because it is exactly what I would put down. If I have to go, let me do it that way. The vision of idleness, and of being a burden overwhelmed me. That is a natural instinct, not wanting to be a burden, and right now it owned me.

That was Lenny Bruce's feeling. "I don't want to put it on you," he always said. He sat up there on the windowsill in my office at the *Herald-Tribune*. I had this conference room that nobody used and I got into it first, Dick Schaap followed and we never gave it up. Sitting up on the windowsill every day was Lenny Bruce, wearing T-shirt, jeans and gaunt face. He drank coffee, chewed Hershey Bars and read these enormous manuscripts of his trial in criminal court. He had been convicted for swearing in a nightclub. Saying fuck in a place that sold whiskey. The district attorney was Frank Hogan, who wanted New York to live by an old Catechism. Today, Hogan would try to electrocute Calvin Klein.

We left the door open so you had the noise and energy of a city room coming right in on you. We typed on old Underwoods and one day my friend Fat Thomas came around. When he looked at Lenny, he saw thirty-five hundred dollars for a nightclub appearance.

"Lenny, what do you got there in the

script, a big part?"

"It's my case," Lenny said. "I am taking it on appeal to the Second Circuit Federal Court. I want to get this to the Supreme Court. This is the First Amendment case of our time. Here, let me read you this."

"Don't start now, I want to get coffee," Fat Thomas said. "Want anything?"

"Coffee and a couple of Hershey Bars," Bruce said. "I don't want to put it on you, but I don't have any money."

He never did. On this day, Fat Thomas was coming in from a hammering out on the broad boulevards of his city. He started for the door and then stopped. "Lenny, you'll do me a favor. You'll take the fucking transcript and throw it out the window. Leave criminal cases to legitimate criminals. You go out and get yourself booked on the fucking stage and come back here with the money."

I will tell you about one night when I should have learned something about how fast a whole life can go. I am on Church Avenue in Brooklyn, in the noise and smoke and shouting of the Madison Democratic Club. It is a large, old storefront. There are Brooklyn women with election-night hair, and men in the hallway talking with tailored suits and bright ties and telling each other that this is going to be such a long night because, what do you expect? it is a primary for mayor. Beame the mayor, up for reelection, comes out of this very clubhouse, started here as a precinct captain, and has just put on a campaign that took years to assemble. Everybody has to stay until he finally wins. At 9:00 P.M. a stillness falls on the room. The polls have just closed. This is now the Hour of Slander. Always, before computers ruined it, campaign workers had a nice hour to sit around between the excitement of the final voting hour and the first returns coming in by phone. During this hour they picked out the person they all decided to blame in case the election goes bad.

And now I hear Monroe Berliner announce, "Do you know why we lost? Max didn't do the job right."

"I never like to say anything bad about anybody," Beadie Markowitz said. "But Max should be ashamed of himself."

She sighed. "I shouldn't be talking like that."

Then she whispered to me in the hall, "When he gets home tonight, Max should go into the bathroom, and take poison."

Then the noise grows louder as people who had been working the streets push in.

Women sit in silence at long tables covered with phones. Soon, the poll watchers will call in with results from the key districts, the ones that will tell everybody whether they have won the election or not. A few feet away from the phone table sits Nat Sobel, the Kings County surrogate, with printed forms for returns from precincts. He has been in this clubhouse since he was fifteen. Now he has been rewarded with the job of surrogate, which in Kings County is a much better job than president of the United States.

At 9:30 P.M., the first phone rings. It rings once, almost softly. Beadie Markowitz, with her fresh-colored light hair, picks it up.

"Quiet! Shut up!"

The whole room is still.

"Yes, Max," she says. "First, before you start. Max, how is your wife? You tell her we all were asking. Now what do you have for me? Uh huh." She writes down numbers on a slip.

"Thank you, Max," she says.

Somebody grabs the slip of paper. "It's ours! Beame wins."

He kisses Beadie Markowitz. "Oh, I love you, I love you."

"We're winning!" somebody else shouts.

"Win!" they all shout.

They hand the slip of paper to Nat Sobel, the old judge. He looks at it.

"We're dead."

He is not heard by a room still screaming in triumph. He quietly explains to me, "See? Beame has 124, Cuomo 115. And Koch at 95. This is Beame's best district. He should win by much, much more. It's not nearly enough. That means in districts where he is not this strong he will lose."

Sobel stood up. "It's over," he said.

"It didn't even start," somebody cries.

Nat Sobel is wandering into the back of the clubhouse for coffee.

"Long night, Nat?" an old guy who stood at the potato salad said.

"It's over," Sobel said.

I thought it was only an election result. Actually, it was a slight demonstration of all of life in about three-sixteenths of a second. And it all goes that fast.

Now I am conducting an examination of conscience. Did you ever pause to do something for somebody else? It is a good question at this time, seeing as you could die and be questioned, or come out as a despised, useless lump and thus unable to help yourself, much less perform some selfless act that would be an asset at death. So did you do anything at all?

I don't know. I look out at the empty street and I think. I am no good and I can prove it. That's easy. But did I ever do anything that turned out good for somebody else?

It is a Friday afternoon and I am in Charlotte, North Carolina, to cover the important collegiate tournament basketball game between New York University and West Virginia.

I had just been told over the phone by my friend Fat Thomas, who was clerking for a bookmaker up in New York, "What do they call this thing? This game moved three points since noon. How could they fix a game without telling us? My people are gettin' incensed."

The boss of the bookmaking office was Cusamano the Snow Man. He was called this because he went door to door on Christmas Eve to collect anything owed to him.

"Raymond, I don't care what we got, please don't touch any money from anybody," I said to Raymond Paprocky on this most important day in his life.

"Never!" Raymond said. He acted like he was wounded.

"Raymond, don't you even talk to anybody you don't know," I said.

Now he is steaming. He is trying to rest before a big college basketball game in which he was supposed to star, and I am accusing him of planning to shoot foul shots that bounce off the rim.

He had $1,500 folded in his pocket right then.

Ray Paprocky came from Woodward Avenue in Ridgewood. He was out of Grover Cleveland High and it seemed he could not be denied a professional career. But money turned his head faster than all the girls he ever saw. There was at this time one Jack Molinas, who had played at Columbia and with the Fort Wayne professional team. All he ever wanted was to be a famous Mafia gangster. He was thrown out of basketball for betting on games. After that, he became a cheap accident lawyer who was paying college players to shave points: Win for your college if you must, but make sure that you win by less than the point spread. Better than that, do it the sure way: Blow the game.

Paprocky fell in with Molinas and took a down payment of fifteen hundred to blow the game here in this big crowded arena in Charlotte. And the game was tied with about twenty-five seconds left. Jerry West of West Virginia had the ball. West became a great professional star. Tom Sanders was guarding him. Sanders went on to play for years and well for the Boston Celtics. West started to the right. Sanders was with him. West nods to the left. Sanders does not move. Here they were, chest to chest, on this last play of the game and now West burst for the basket left foot first and Sanders had his hands up all right but West was, what, an eighth of a step, a quarter step ahead? It was just enough to give West a clear look at the basket and he was gathering himself to get up there and suddenly a hand came out from nowhere. It came out just enough to interfere with West and he tried to climb in the air over the hand but he could not. He had to take a bad shot that missed because of that hand in the way.

The hand was Raymond Paprocky's, who in the end could not serve a gambler. Then NYU went to win in overtime, 82–81.

I don't know what he did with the money. I think he gave it back to Molinas. There were enough stories around to keep Paprocky from thinking of the pros. When he finished school that year, he took the New York Fire Department exam, but then Molinas was arrested, and Paprocky was turned down by the Fire Department.

I had a couple of beers with Paprocky in a bar on the corner of Woodward and Onderdonk in Ridgewood and he said quietly, "I never saw fifteen hundred before."

I knew exactly what he meant and it absolved him of nothing that he did. He could have had an important career in the professional league and that was denied him forever. He had taken the money, no question. At that last second he saved himself with character that sprang spontaneously. As the good always have something to hope for, he wanted to be on the Fire Department.

I don't know when it was exactly, maybe a year later, but I was at a fire in the old, crowded Bushwick section of Brooklyn, and I thought of Paprocky. The fire was in an old frame building that once had been a mayonnaise factory. It had been turned into a four-story dwelling with so many in each apartment that people slept on the floor.

The wood on the ground floor was soaked with years of mayonnaise grease. It went up like a stack of old newspapers. People were trapped on the fire escape in the rear and the flames coming from below broiled them like they were on a griddle. I guess a half dozen died. And I could imagine Raymond Paprocky's fast hands grabbing people off the fire escape.

I was standing on the street with Raymond Nolan, a deputy chief. I told him about Paprocky. When he made a face about the basketball scandal, I said, "What does some game that never happened have to do with pulling people off the fire escape back there?"

Then I met Nolan at a dinner and I was half stewed and felt like a field marshal. This was when I was starting to do all right in my business and I told Nolan, "I vouch personally for the guy. Handle it."

I forgot all about it. Then I was home early one morning when the phone rang. It was Chief Nolan. "I am reading the Fire Department orders for the day," he said. " 'Retiring. Deputy Chief Raymond Nolan. Appointed as probationary fire fighter, Raymond Paprocky.' "

Then he said, "It took me right to the last day to get it done. But I did."

I never called Paprocky. Wasn't it better to let him forget we ever knew each other? And I never saw him even by accident again. But my emotion had been correct, and my judgment on those hands of his was even better. One morning the newspaper came up with a big headline about firefighter Raymond Paprocky taking a desperate chance and saving people in a fire in Queens. I figured Nolan saw it, too. I never called him, either. I saw his name one other time.

There was a story about his son, a good high school player, who was about to go away to college. When asked about his father, the son fiercely defended him.

7

9:20: Pt. arrived to BNI-O.R. per cart, awake and alert. Pleasant and cooperative, no distress noted. Pre-op nurse, Pacheco, Daria, RN.

SURGICAL CONSENT: Pt. verbalizes understanding of procedure and wishes to proceed. DP.

"I'm glad to see you looking so good," the first nurse to come up to me said when I was pushed through the flying doors and into the operating room.

I remember that I thought that they just pushed you into an operating room, but from what I could see now there were several of them. The crowd of green, the doctors and nurses, were in the one hallway and at the end of it, they were walking to and from rooms on either side.

The cart I was on now was stopped.

"Do you have any allergies?" the nurse said to me.

"No."

"Good." She was writing on a clipboard.

"What's your name?" I asked her.

"Pacheco. Daria Pacheco. Have you had surgery before?"

"No. What time did you start this morning?"

"I was here at 6:30. Do you have any implants?"

"No. You married?"

"I am a single mother. When was the last time you had anything to eat and drink?"

"Early last night. You got kids in school?"

"My daughter. I bring her to St. Francis before I come here. You know you are going to have brain surgery?"

"I sure do."

"Do you wish to proceed?"

"Absolutely."

She put a form in front of me and I signed it. She was moving around me now and not too interested in what I had to say. Dr. Raudzens took my arm and with very little motion put a needle right into it on the first jab. Then he hooked a tubing running to the needle up on a coat hanger. That was it. A smile that it was done. We were on the very verge of a profound act and this was like a common vaccination.

Dripping into my arm was two milligrams of Versed. This is a new form of Valium. It is much quicker and lasts longer.

If I had been using drugs or a lot of alcohol, the liver would have had a buildup of enzymes to metabolize the drug quickly. But I have never even taken a puff of marijuana in my life. And I have not had a strong drink in what, two years?

So the drug sailed silently through my blood and had to come through nothing.

Watching me, Dr. Peter Raudzens, who was there to administer the serious drugs, was pleasantly surprised at how quickly it went. The night before, I had assured him that I did not drink anymore and now I began proving it right in front of him.

Pre-Op Notes:
FROM: 11/22/94 at 9:20:
NURSING DX: Potential for knowledge deficit/anxiety related to surgical intervention.
GOAL: Demonstrates knowledge/decreased anxiety.
PRE-OP NOTES:
-0-

I am rolling down another hallway and there was a doorway and a man in a gown stood in a doorway of a lighted room and talked to a large man in a short-sleeved blue shirt who held *Newsweek* magazine. A nurse

312

sat and read a book by J. D. Salinger.

"Just a moment, I have Carol Blazier here," she says.

Carol Blazier stands alongside her. She is wrapped in blue surgical clothes, her hair covered with a shower hat. She has her arms folded so she won't touch anything. The other nurse holds the phone up to Carol Blazier.

"That's common. Then he'll spit up. Scrub his nose when he does."

She nods and the other nurse puts the phone back. Carol Blazier walks away through water.

Another nurse is on the phone. She had her wedding ring on a safety pin pinned to her green blouse. She fingers the ring in the safety pin as she talks.

"Fine, but what time do you think we ought to get there? I'll be hungry before that. What should we do. Go for pizza somewh— ?"

There is a grind, a whine, a high loud whine that goes through the air.

The nurse says, "All right. I'll call back."

She hangs up. "My husband goes crazy when he hears this sound. . . ."

There was a small man with dark eyebrows and sharp look with his blue operating gown wrapped around him and coming to his ankles and another man with an intense look and dark eyebrows. And that is the end of memory. Without sound or the slightest sensation, I was out without knowing it. They now decide my life without me.

I was pushed into an operating room I never saw and Peter Raudzens started Diprivan and a synthetic narcotic called sufentanyl dripping into me, and another drug called vecuronium that stills all muscles. That was enough to stall a truck.

"We did that right away, one after the other," Raudzens reports. "There is no waiting around. We're committed. The plane is taking off."

My brain was present, but the mind that lives in it plunged through dusk and into a night I would never recall.

I became a body on a table for brain surgery.

Details now come from 501 pages of notes that were written or dictated by doctors and nurses and placed on a computer at the hospital, covering everything, including the minute I was wheeled into the operating room. And also from the pictures taken during the operation by Pam for use in medical lectures. These pages and pictures then were discussed with some of the doctors and nurses. The medical people involved all have extraordinary memories and the orderly mind to tell a story that is found in those who do emergency work. They also have a subject in which I have a slight interest.

So they told me what happened to me and I tell you promptly and thus prominently:

INTRAOPERATIVE ASSESSMENT
SURGEON 1 SPETZLER, ROBERT F.
SURGEON 2 MORCOS, JACQUES
CIRCULATOR: PACHECO, DARIA

POSITIONING DEVICES: In supine position with head on 3-point Mayfield headrest. Right arm foam padded and tucked on side. Left arm on foam-padded armboard. Extra foam padding to all pressure points. Pillow under knees and lower legs.
Pt. carefully taped onto O.R. table.

OTHER O.R. STAFF: Joyce Schlichting, M.D./Anesthesia Resident; Jim Higgins, REEGT/EPT.

OTHER O.R. EQUIPMENT: Midas Rex drill.
Zeiss scope and chair.
SSEP and CSA monitoring.

Implanted in O.R.: Walter Lorenz 4-hole plates X5
Walter Lorenz 5mm screws X10.
-0-

There were seven in the operating room.

The operation was listed as right pterinonal craniotomy with clipping of unruptured anterior communicating artery aneurysm. The right pterinonal refers to a ridge that separates the middle and front of the brain.

From 9:20 A.M. until 10:30 A.M. on this morning, November 22, they work to set me up properly on the operating table. My head had to be in what Spetzler considered perfect orientation to the aneurysm. While the body was on the table, the head was hanging off and was held by three pins of a device called a Mayfield clamp. The head had to be rotated to the precise angle needed to take the skull bone off and go into the brain. The right cheekbone had to be the highest point.

"That gives you a direct shot. A flat shot behind the eye," one of the residents explained.

The right cheekbone being on high also caused the brain to fall away from the skull.

The position of the body required no pressure on the arms or legs. I was covered with a blue foamy material that looked like the inside of a crate of eggs.

While my head was being set, there were intravenous lines put into the internal jugular vein in my neck and into the arm. They ran drugs into me and checked blood pressure and heartbeat.

They had me on an operating table. There was another table placed atop that served as a desk. A nurse sat on a high stool on the right side. On the table in front of her was one of the sets of twelve hundred tools used in surgery on brains. Her job was to hand people instruments with virtually no conversation.

A blue magic marker was used to draw a line all across the top of the forehead, right behind the hairline. Somebody took a needle and scratched marks along the line as an insurance guideline. A nurse had spread a blue towel on the pale yellow floor so the hair would fall on it and could be picked up and disposed of easily. They had shaved only minimal hair from the front. They had not shaved my whole head. Which was meaningless to me awake or unconscious. I still remember my friend Eppie Lederer, who writes in Chicago under the name of

Ann Landers, standing in front of a woman who was in tears because she was losing her hair from chemotherapy treatments. "The hell with the hair. Get a wig. Let's concentrate on staying alive." Another towel was put down to catch blood.

The nurses now scrubbed the skin with Betadine, an iodine solution that colors the skin a dirty yellow. They used blue towels to define the surgical field. The towels were folded around the area to be cut open. Folded exactly the same as in every operation. The routine is always the same, to soften the moments with familiarity as much as possible.

The doctor at my head touched me under the hairline with a Number 10 Bard-Parker blade. The blade is disposable. He cut to the bone with this thin scalpel. He cut only the top of the skin at the gum-chewing muscles on the sides, the temporalis and masseter muscles. He had two hinge points at the temples. Now he cut what looked like a circle route on an airlines map. A great C, following the hairline across the forehead to the right temple and then came down a little, even with the ear top.

The scalp has five layers. It is made of skin, connective tissue, poneuroisis, loose connective tissue and pericranium, which covers the skull. When the incision was made, gloved hands gently took the skin of my forehead and pulled it down over my eyes. The skin bunched up in folds, like a drape. Now two doctors threaded lines through the top fold of skin and they ran the lines up to the top of my forehead, into whatever scalp was left, and they anchored each thread with what looked like a fish hook. The lines were anchored to a Lele bar, a heavy metal bar attached to the side of the operating table and running across my neck like a chinning bar. They did this twice more, three times more and soon there were nine lines, anchored by nine fish hooks in the very top of my scalp that were holding my skin up so that it would not roll up any more.

It is a face that is thirsty for rain. Sunlight striking a blade of grass always causes me to feel empty and instantly depressed. I look up into a rain, a heavy rain that comes out of the sky white and hard, and my eyes squint and perhaps close for an instant against the water rolling off the eyebrows. It is a face that has looked up into cold driving rainstorms on a February night in New York. And has been sprayed and splashed on the Sheepshead, a cliff ten stories over the cold Atlantic in Ireland. The charcoal gray waves slap loudly against the rocks at the bottom of the cliff and heavy white spray leaps high into the air and into your face. It has looked straight up into the torrent of warm white water coming out of the sky each afternoon in Saigon.

And now I do not have my face on me. They took the face off me like it was wrapping paper.

The face that looked into rain, or that searched the faces of my children and tried to see if they looked like me, and I couldn't tell because no matter how often I use a mirror I really don't know what I look like, this face now was gone. Instead the light gleams on a white skull.

I had no more face. I was a live skeleton.

Inside the skull, an aneurysm sat like a loaded gun at the front of my brain.

In the far right corner of the room, there was a black tank strapped to an aluminum cart. The tank was filled with nitrogen and was the kind welders always have next to them in an auto body shop. It had a six-foot-long green hose, two inches in diameter, coming out of it that was connected to a large brass head that was covered with clear thick plastic wrapping. The brass head, big as both your fists together, sat separately on a small table, the light making it seem lustrous, a treasure just pulled from the sea bottom.

A nurse went to the corner of the room and put the brass head on top of the tank and dragged the gas tank over to the table, taking it from an auto repair garage and into the bright weirdness and unseen vapors of the supernatural.

They had my face. Now they were going behind that to look for my brain.

A Jimi Hendrix tape came over a speaker. "The Star-Spangled Banner" from Woodstock.

Spetzler came in from a cup of coffee. He has coffee every morning. He remembers that the night before he had gone over the case and had thought about the potential for problems, and he prepared himself for a surprise. The shape of the aneurysm first. It could be much different from the two-dimensional angiogram film. He reminded himself of all the surprises and how he had handled them. Now when he arrived for his operation in the chill room in the morning, he understood that there is nothing that he cannot do. He is the best of his time at his specialty, which was the aneurysm in front of him.

He went between people without grazing them and directly to the head of the table, without a sound. He does not wear paper booties over his shoes. They take too much time to put on and take off all day. He has three pairs of identical ivory-colored leather loafers that are treated with silicone. The blood gets washed off, and he goes on.

He was supremely confident. Jimi Hendrix has gone off the speaker and now a classical music tape is being played.

"What is the name of the piece and the composer?" Spetzler remembers asking.

The young doctors, the residents working with him, do not answer. They look at each other.

"Come on," Spetzler says. "You people have European educations. Don't embarrass me in front of him."

Although I am not so alert at this moment.

Nobody answers. "It is 'The Trout Quintet.' The composer is Schubert," he says.

The room was a square. Three television monitors hang from the ceiling in the corners. Soon, they would turn on a camera and put the inside of my head up live on big screens. There was one window, looking out at a sink in the hallway. The door was open. There were cabinet drawers opening, trays being put down someplace, the sound of casters rolling across the floor.

At the table, Spetzler holds a drill that is at the end of the black hose. The drill runs at 180,000 RPMs and he holds it to the off-white skull that has been left exposed by the skin hanging on fish hooks. He operates the drill speed with his foot. The Midas Rex saw looks like a heavy fountain pen with a line attached to it that goes to the black tank of gas. The high-speed saw screams through the antiseptic room as he drills. Now, in the cool and darkness, the one light coming from the ceiling picks out the cloud of bone dust as the saw bites into the skull. The saw has such speed that it turns skull bone into dust instead of splinters that could fly into the brain. The skull has a near-foul smell to it that comes when a dentist drills a rotted tooth. The doctor standing on Spetzler's right holds a large plastic tube, with a rubber bulb. He squeezes the bulb and water bathes the area. Man basting a turkey. He keeps doing this quickly, so that the drilling was heavily irrigated with water that rushed the bone dust away as sludge. It was sucked up by a hose.

He drills a burr hole, a small hole in the skull at the top of the head. That's how they start, like ice fishing.

The skull is between two and three centimeters thick. The drilling goes for a burst of twenty seconds first. It sounds like an hour. In Peru, where they are supposed to descend from ignorant Indians crouched in the dust like insects, there are old skulls with holes in them that show that the man with the skull lived past the long hours when the holes were made, and that the bone had grown together somewhat, proving the man had lived for at least a while. The shaven bone shows that they forced and scraped with a dagger until the hole was open. They were called trephination holes because they were made with a hand-held trephine, which was a screwdriver. Turn and twist. Carpenter at work on a barn.

The Incas in Peru hoped that whatever was ailing the poor guy would pour out of his head and relieve him. Often, they took a man with a throbbing headache and put him in a corner and stuffed his mouth with coca leaves. He chewed himself daffy. If the headache persisted, they figured he had a real problem, and was also high enough on coca to withstand some drilling. Today, helicopter gunships would chase the coca chewer. As so many skulls with holes in them indicated, whatever they did with a dagger sometimes was successful.

By the 1970s, they called the tool a Codman perforator. You drilled four holes with it, then passed a giggley, a wire with saw-teeth, through one hole and under the skull bone and out the other hole and then started sawing from underneath with the motion of a logger. You connect the four holes with the sawing and just lift the piece of skull out like a cutout from a holiday pumpkin.

And now here is this new high-speed drill whining and shrieking as it sends the cloud of dust. The drill coming into my skull has a footplate that curves around the drill bit. The drill bit comes down to the cuff of the footplate. The drill cannot plunge any deeper than the cuff. This prevents the drill from going right on into the brain.

An entry point is next. The whine stops. They change the drill bit to use one that makes the precise room needed to go under the skull flap and inside. The whine picks up and he saws through an opening in my skull.

There are two bony hard surfaces to the skull, with a soft middle. The Midas Rex drill makes such a loud sound as it saws the skull bone that some surgeons wear ear-muffs, as if working on an airline ground crew.

Spetzler saws a three-inch by four-inch oval in the skull. He lifts the piece out of the skull. The color of the bone is shiny ivory white. He places the piece of skull on the edge of the table and covers it with a sterilized blue cloth.

The brain of which I write is watertight. Skin so loving of rain is only the outer wall of a dike. The brain is wrapped in two layers, one tough, the dura mater, which stands for "tough mother," and under that the pia mater, or "soft mother," which is a thin film directly covering the brain. Between the layers is brain fluid that has to be suctioned to let the brain relax. There is no worry about replacement. The brain continuously produces spinal fluid. Spetzler peels the dura back to the pia.

The brain itself feels no pain. You can plunge a dagger into it and nothing hurts. You don't leave very much alive, but what there is left does not hurt.

The brain is pink on the surface, running to gray coiled vessels underneath. Red lines running through the pink-white surface are arteries that feed the parts of the brain that control all of life. Touch an artery and the person on the table instantly loses entire sections of his life.

My life is exactly in the hands, and the guy doesn't even know who I am when he meets me.

8

DOCUMENT 39333

11/22/94

OPERATIVE PROCEDURE: Right frontal temporal craniotomy clipping of anterior communicating artery, unruptured aneurysm with placement of a small cottonball around the unclipped portion.

DETAILS OF THE PROCEDURE: With the patient intubated and under a general anesthesia, placed supine with the head turned to the left and extended, a C shaped incision was made from the root of the zygoma to the middle of the hairline down to bone and the myocutaneous flap was retracted anteriorly. A free bone flap was taken with a single burrhole, covering the frontotemporal area. The lesser wing of the splenoid was drilled generously down to the floor of the anterior fossa and then the dura was tacked up and opened in a C shaped fashion. The microscope was brought in and subfrontal retraction was started down to the olfactory tract and the optic nerve and CSF was sucked from the opticocarotid cistern. We immediately identified an A1 and followed it medially until we reached the anterior interhemispheric fissure which was opened and identified the right A1, the right A2 and the left A1.

-0-

My brain sits like a chalice on an altar of clean blue cloth. It needs no body. The rest of my body cannot be seen, not even the head. The brain is detached from everything and is alone in the light on the end of this table. The sight of it halts the words in your throat. Only the priests speak in its presence.

When the brain speaks, it says clearly in a silent room: Touch me and I put death on your hands.

Yet it has a garish appearance that at first looks like a beaded purse left open, or a pop advertisement of a gaudy mouth. The lips are decorated with purple beads that are placed close together all around the oval opening, which is about six inches long and wide. Large red gums billow just inside the lips and then curve away, the bottom going down and quickly out of sight and the top curving upwards, in exact reverse.

The purple beads are called Rainey clips. They hold the edges of the skin around the opening together to prevent bleeding. If the skin bleeds and dies, there will not be enough skin to cover the hole when they try to close it up. Any open hole can be a liability in inclement weather.

You can't see any part of me because I am draped with sterilized blue. The head of the body is also draped in blue and all that shows is the oval opening into the brain with its ring of purple beads. The operating nurse sits halfway down the right side of the table with packs of instruments folded inside blue sterilized cloth which she knows like the tune of a song when to open and when to hand across to the surgeon.

Who stares into the brain with a doctor on his right arm, another on his left.

And now you are where life lives.

The room was dim and the temperature kept low, as cold as a meat locker. Now Spetzler sits on a chair that looks like it came from an expensive barber shop. He operated the height and tilt of the chair with his feet. In his mouth he had the switch to the large Zeiss microscope. The scope enlarges and illuminates so that he is looking at a large, bright map. The scope also throws what it sees onto large wall monitors for the rest of the surgeons to watch. The microscope comes out of the armaments industry where heavy guns could be moved by a single person with a counterbalance switch. Spetzler has the same switch between his teeth as he directs the heavy microscope. He keeps his hands free.

The brain is firm smooth white with red lines running through it. There is the light evil dental smell. Would the inside of a saint's head smell sweet? The first thing Spetzler does is make certain that he is ready for a rupture. He does not expect one, but you must prepare to defeat the worst before you proceed to the mere threatening. At his left hand is a silver rod made of coils, operated by a handle. On the end of the rod is what looks like a butter knife. The blade on both sides has the same covering as used on the back of Band-Aids. Operating this rod by hand, Spetzler causes the rod to uncoil a little, to extend, and place the retractor against the brain and gently push the lobes of the brain apart. The retractor blade also protects the brain from the instruments that are coming in. As the brain has no feeling of pain, any pain that comes out of an operation is either "in your thin scalp or thick skull," Peter Raudzens said.

Spetzler's hands speak to him of how much pressure to use. He inherited a watchmaker's hands that can work on tiny things, and do it for hours. And he was born with a stillness in his hands that becomes complete as tension heightens, as they work nearer and nearer to the flesh and tiny little hairs that are arteries and can cause calamities and death at the very touch. A tranquillity settles over the hands. You can beg your heart to be still, and it never really listens until the romance, the threat, the triumph that excites it has disappeared. But when you work at the gates of life, stillness is the prerequisite.

A neurosurgeon can attend schools for a decade and learn all of science to do with the brain. But let there be one shake on the job and he is gone and so are you. And that is the job description.

Extraordinary depth perception also develops in the crib or there is no surgeon. Spetzler must immediately identify the vessels as they branched off from the area from which the aneurysm was arising. If the aneurysm ruptures, the blood would come out of it so quickly as to be paralyzing to watch.

Still, he remembers being in the Veterans Hospital in San Francisco and opening up a man who had a skull fracture, but whose scans showed no bleeding. Suddenly the blood came from everywhere.

"I knew that the first thing I should do was just stop. One hurried move would have made the thing fatal. Just hold yourself together and think. Then proceed. I was able to get the man out of it."

Of course everybody does not. His is the busiest neurosurgery operating room in the country, with the Mayo Clinic second. They come in wheelchairs and ask to be sent home walking. There is no risk too big for that. They come with tumors so deep and so large that no one else would go in after them. And so always there is a patient getting dressed to go home after a tumor operation and the pupil on the left side suddenly balloons. "Doc," one says to resident Jonathan Baskin. "Something bad is going on inside." Suddenly there is blood everywhere. The skull tumor has eaten away one carotid artery and now the other blew. There is a huge bleed and the patient goes home in a box.

Working on me in these moments now, he has to know and be ready to seal off all the vessels around the aneurysm that would feed blood to the aneurysm. He uses a bi-polar, which has purple plastic handles and two prongs that make it look like the pliers I fear, except that when he brings them close together a current spits out. Anything between is seared and smoky and cauterized.

Somewhere in the midst of this, he looks at a vein and said, "All this can do is bleed. We'll vaporize it." He holds the bipolars to the vein and sets it afire. The vein curls into a cinder and smoke comes out of my brain.

If the aneurysm burst, there would be blood spurting from the rupture without end, spilling and killing cells. Blood on the brain is most toxic.

There are fourteen vessels that must be identified and checked immediately. Some are so tiny to the eye as to seem completely innocuous. But all have the potential to destroy a brain and body, and even the entire life, at a touch.

That first surgeon ever to do aneurysms, Walter Dandy, recounted in 1920 that he operated on a patient who was awake. He brushed the floor of the fourth ventricle with a bit of wet cotton and the patient stopped breathing right there and had a cardiac arrest. Dandy said in wonder, "Never have I seen a patient die so quickly and quietly."

The only people who keep time during this operation are the families waiting outside. Here at the table, forty-five minutes pass without a murmur, with the hands picking silently at the brain inside that circle of purple clips.

He looks for the optic nerve, which is around the midline at the front of the brain. On the microscope it is a white pearly structure. There it is; that's how you see things through your whole life. Touch that nerve and you go blind right now. The optic nerve is Nature's utmost effort. It allows the wonders of sight and at the same time is so maddeningly delicate and frightfully dangerous. "I could see it in his eyes," they write of a person's emotions showing. Of course this is a fable told by someone in need of a paragraph. Eyes alight; eyes in fright. My eyes now are under the blue cloth and reflect this slender thread buried in the brain behind the eyes. If it moves, shrivels or suddenly has something press against it, then forever the eyes will only know black night.

The optic nerve is also the landmark that marks the start of surgery on an aneurysm. What looks like a spiderweb is a street map to Spetzler. There are boulevards and side streets and he begins with his Broadway, the optic nerve. There is a thin membrane, the arachnoid, that covers and obscures the map and must be cut away in order for him to see more of the avenues and streets. The cutting is done with tiny scissors at the end of long handles that slope down to the scissors so that the instrument doesn't block the sight.

With the optic nerve as a wide street, the eye moves to the carotid artery, which looks like a forearm on the microscope. Once that is identified, the retractors are moved and follow back to the artery labeled as A1 in the operating notes. The crossbar on the A is the anterior communicating artery, where the aneurysm is hanging.

This is part of what is named the Circle of Willis, which runs blood around the brain. If blood is interrupted on one side, the circle diverts it to the other side. Nobody has the same alignment of blood vessels around the brain. It is almost like fingerprints. In my case, the left side as you face it is not there. This is my anomaly. Instead of artery lines, there is only a gloomy emptiness. The heavy run of blood needed for the brain came up the right side of my brain as you faced it.

DETAILS OF THE PROCEDURE: The aneurysm was immediately seen, pointing essentially downward towards the optic chiasm but certainly not touching it. It was about

6 mm in size. We did not have, at first, an immediate view of the left A2. However, after dissecting the aneurysm off the vessels, we identified the left A2 at the depths. It became clear that the aneurysm had actually two lobes and even a small nubbin that was taken out of the anterior communicating artery posteriorly, with a group of hypothalamic perforators.

Spetzler peered through a microscope. The brain was exposed and he could see down a dark valley to the aneurysm. Which no longer was this compact bulge that was seen on a two-dimensional MRI or angiogram film.

Of course Spetzler had thought about this the night before, an aneurysm that gave a surprise, but even with this preparation, and all this experience, he dropped his arms to his sides and remembers saying, "Mamma Mia." Always something meaningless.

He was alone with an opponent.

The aneurysm was two. The top of each of them was as wide as the neck. They were dark red but the outer part was so thin that it changed to purple. It was like a balloon filled to the point of bursting. The blood swirled around inside the aneurysm with each of my heartbeats and this could be seen by Spetzler through the thin wall of the aneurysm.

He was defusing a bomb that could go off without even ticking.

The aneurysm was draped with tiny blood vessels that resembled hairs. One of them was so much more than that. It was a tiny vessel that went back, curving like a snake, from the aneurysm to the area of the brain that gives you speech and the ability to put words on paper. The reason medical people can say something like this with assuredness is that there have been many hundreds of thousands of people who have had strokes in that area and came out unable to speak or write much more than their names.

Before wars made the microscope he used, surgeons came to these tiny threads and, barely able to see what they were, simply went for the aneurysm. The threads, the tiny blood vessels, were snipped and if any blood showed the thread was cauterized and left hanging. And the patient went out of the hospital and back to work. Where he could not even begin to write a memo or react to the phone ringing. He immediately lost the promotion he had been after. A month later he was demoted from the job he had, and was transferred to the elevator starter's job.

Right now, all that I was born with, whatever it is I can do, clings on this one tiny curving strand, thread, filum.

And the fingertips of Robert Spetzler are so close to that filum. He is alone now, which is the only way he wants it and the only way he has ever had it.

He is five and in Würzburg and he steps on a rusty nail and develops tetanus. The toxins attack his system and he is put into a terminal ward. All the other children in the ward were in iron lungs. Spetzler is kept in the terminal ward because the doctors don't want other children in the hospital to be upset when he dies. Then a doctor came in with a medicine called penicillin, which had been brought around by American troops. Spetzler spent weeks in grave condition until the penicillin worked.

Now he is in front of a large auditorium filled with medical students and he is being presented as a case of someone who had tetanus and survived with this new penicillin.

They talk about him indifferently. Just a case. And he is all alone and he begins to concentrate on the scene. The students, the professor explaining the medicine. He is only five and he is in his first deep trance.

Through the hours of small movements in places where hands could touch nothing,

Spetzler lived in this deep concentration.

The neuro-anesthesiologist, Peter Raudzens, now put barbiturates into my vein to put the brain into a coma. This was done to reduce the brain's requirement for oxygen and energy. He used bacitracin, an antibiotic, 50,000 units, thrombin, a coagulant, 1,000 units, Xylocaine, an anti-arrhythmia drug, papaverine, 30 mg, to keep blood vessels dilated.

The electrodes attached to my head recorded the entire operation. At the far end of the table, Raudzens and Jim Higgins, an electroencephalogram technician, were at a heart monitor and an EEG tape. They tapped a computer. Stretches of raw EEG tape were printed on a printer that barely hummed. This faint tapping and low electronic squeals were normal in a room of murmurs. The computer was charting the brain waves. The records show that first Raudzens had the computer show him the Compressed Spectral Array display. This was an examination of spontaneous electrical waves from the brain. The display showed symmetrical power from both hemispheres. This meant both sides of the brain were having equal blood flow. That tends to be necessary if you are going to come out of this thinking.

The other test Raudzens kept running was one that generated nervous system responses. It was called the Somatosensory Evoked Responses. One electrode sent an electrical signal into the medial nerve of the wrist. This signal runs up the wrist and to the spinal dorsal column and right up to the sensory cortex. Either it is recorded on the brain waves in 20 milliseconds or there is trouble.

The barbiturates had caused my blood to walk through my body. Now at this one point when Spetzler wanted stillness, the barbiturates caused the blood walk to stop at a corner for a red light.

DETAILS OF THE PROCEDURE: It became clear that this aneurysm whole complex could not be clipped with one clip and we were satisfied in placing a straight clip through both the domes and leaving the small nubbin posteriorly.

Now, Spetzler said, "All right, no talking please. Only if you have to. Thank you."

Suddenly the room was still and he went into a trance. "You would think that your aneurysm was talking to him," Dr. Raudzens said.

His body still, his concentration total, he

held pliers. A silver clip that was six millimeters long was in the pliers. It was just
long enough to clip the aneurysm but not
too long to obstruct the vessels around it.

Spetzler, in his trance, worked on the
aneurysm with two heads. It had no neck.
The tops were as wide as the body. Therefore, he had no way to place the permanent
silver clip. He used two temporary clips to
trap the aneurysm. During his probing, the
aneurysm tore open — the temporary clips
won't hold it. The clip is a tiny piece of
titanium that opens up like jaws. But the
human hand can't get them open. The pliers
are needed. He worked for forty minutes on
this. Time never counts.

And now the aneurysm suddenly moved.
It was twisted and soft and with two heads
and the blood was swirling and it all seemed
to move right up at Spetzler. Suddenly,
there was danger that had not shown on
angiogram film. And it was at this moment
that Spetzler's life and ability came together.
The hands you trust with your life get their
confidence for the same reason that you
place yours in them. They have the experience that allows them to stare at danger,
and take any measure to suppress it, out to
the most daring, and walk away with another success.

What I want for all of my life right now is somebody with total arrogance in his own ability. If the guy is not certain to the bones of his body that he is performing right at this instant with skill that can be matched nowhere, and that if something goes wrong then it is entirely my fault on the table, then he is of no use in an emergency like this. I must dismiss him. How would you like, at this moment, a brain surgeon standing over your open head and saying, in lovely, modest tones, "I think I can do it. I'll really try."

I have over me a man who gets up at medical conferences and tells the audience that not only can he do certain things, but that he can do them better than anybody here in the hall.

Now he works with hands that do not seem to move. There are only slight motions of probes and suctions and knives. It is different when seen through the microscope, and on the television screens around the room. Here the aneurysm is the size of a walnut, the hands are pronounced and their work is massive and maddening. With quick little motions, a Penfield probe strikes one of the necks of the two-headed aneurysm. The neck gives. The probe now pushes from the side. The side gives. Suddenly, at the precise moment of more fast small probing, the aneurysm rocks and the color goes from purple to red and the neck inflates all the way around. Start again. Sometime, somehow, the thing must hold its new shape so that it can be killed with a clip. And all the while, through all the probes, all the anxiety, all the tediousness, one law rules the room: Touch me and I will die.

People wander into the operating room. A doctor from Italy, somebody remembers. One from another hospital. They watch the actual work, but mostly stand in front of one large screen and wear 3-D glasses as they watch the operation in depth and color. Spetzler looked at the aneurysm and decided the thickness and searched for any surprise that could lurk behind it. The aneurysm was larger, softer, and twisted. He worked on the aneurysm for over two and a half hours.

His was the bowed head to which all other bowed heads deferred.

He complains. Nurse Carol Blazier remembers him saying, "I don't know what you're wiping these instruments with, but whatever it is, it leaves a glaze on them."

He sighs and steps back. A nurse massages his shoulders.

He relaxes. "Who invented this?" he asks the room, as he holds up an instrument. Nobody answers. "I did that when I was an attending. I thought getting a patent was immoral."

Spetzler was working at setting the clip at the base of the aneurysm. "That was almost perfect," he said. Which meant he was going to start all over again.

Finally, with a twist of his wrist the pliers placed the clip at the base of the shaped aneurysm. The clip closed and choked off the ballooning part of the aneurysm. A needle went into the bulge and the blood came out and was immediately sucked up. There were small pieces of cotton placed around the clip to cause a scar tissue in the artery, strengthening the outer wall. The aneurysm now was gone.

Spetzler reached for the piece of white skull. He fitted it back into the skull like the last brick in a wall. Two miniature hinges now had to be put into the skull by a resident using a screwdriver. The idea is, if they have to go back in someday, there will be none of this screaming sawing. You'll open my skull like a front gate.

That was it. He straightens and says, "Thank you very much." And he walks out for his next operation.

DETAILS OF THE PROCEDURE: We were satisfied with the Yasargil clip that was placed and the arteries were not stenosed and the perforators completely spared and we placed a tiny piece of cotton around the posterior nubbin to encourage wrapping by scar and achieved hemostasis. We closed the dura water tight and replaced the bone flap with central tackups and Lorenz screw and plate system and closed the muscle and galea with Vicryl and placed staples on the skin.

The patient tolerated the procedure very well.

My wife and daughter Rosemary had started the day by getting to the hospital at 7:00 A.M. My wife recalls, "JB was in bed, quite relaxed. We packed his clothes because the nurse said he would not come back to this room. After the operation, he would be taken to the recovery room and then to the Intensive Care Unit. Shortly after eight, an energetic and reassuring nurse arrived to take JB to the operating room. She said she would keep us informed of his progress and suggested we go to the waiting room down the corridor. She thought he would be in the recovery room till about 2:00 P.M.

"Rosemary and I went to the visiting room. It was triangular shaped with windows opening to the corridor. There were couches, several tables and chairs, a sink, coffee machine and a desk manned by a volunteer. The room was already filled with families of patients waiting the outcome of the surgery. We sat next to Mr. Gerson, eighty years old, and his daughter Wendy, who were waiting to hear of Mrs. Gerson's back operation. Mr. Gerson's grandson, Brett, played several games, changed the television stations, drew cartoon strips and talked to us about life, politics and Phoenix.

"There was one telephone in the corner between two sofas where we could make outgoing phone calls. A family from Idaho sat on the couches waiting hours for news of their daughter's/wife's brain tumor operation.

"Also sitting there was a handsome woman from England with her elegant friend from Canada and beautiful daughter-in-law from Singapore. Her son had been operated on the day before for an AVM (arterial venous malformation) and was to spend the next two weeks in the Intensive Care Unit.

"Emily Eldridge arrived at noon. She came directly from the airport and quickly became involved with us in these personal dramas. Periodically, the phone on the volunteer's desk would ring. Everybody would stop talking to listen. She would look at her

346

list, never look around, and only after hanging the phone up would she look up and talk to the family, reporting the progress of the operation. We received our report at about half after twelve. The volunteer reported, "All went well. They were getting ready to close. Then he'll get to Recovery and be brought to ICU around two." As always the room became silent and then the sighs and smiles came when they heard the report.

"Rosemary and Emily went for coffee and something to eat. Shortly after, Dr. Morcos, the senior resident who had worked on the operation, came to see us. He told us the operation was more complicated than expected. The aneurysm was larger, softer and twisted. But everything went well. He also said that he did the closing. That news did not distress me even though everyone in New York had warned us to be sure that Dr. Spetzler did the opening, operation and closing himself. They kept emphasizing the dangers that occur during the whole operation. There was such an aura of assurance and confidence in this hospital that you knew everything done was intentional, planned and successful.

"We were anxious for Jimmy to come to ICU because we could see him when he was there. Two o'clock came, no call. By 3:30 I asked the volunteer to call. She refused, telling me they'd call when they were ready. For a moment it seemed as if all the good feelings had been replaced by gross dissatisfaction and fear. Finally, at around 4:00 P.M., the phone rang and the volunteer nodded, hung up and told us to go down the hall to the Intensive Care Unit and see Jimmy."

My daughter Rosemary remembers: "There were five different groups there at the start of the morning, and I think a turnover of one group while we were there. Everybody started out the same, but once a group got a call, they were looked at differently. The family near us got a good call and as much as I liked them, you were mad at them because you were in limbo. I remember the volunteer at the desk called me over to give me information and when she said 'she' I thought she was talking about the wrong patient, which she was. I can't remember much of what she said, but it was not great news and I was glad it wasn't mine.

"The room was only for the families of people being operated on so the whole group of probably seventeen people were there for the same thing. The big deal was after the phone call or either before or after the doctor's arrival, the patient's family would go out in the hall to see the patient being wheeled from the operating room to Intensive Care. It was the big thrill after all these hours, the minimum of which was roughly four with no word. Some people waited six and seven hours just for the surgery. There was a phone on the corner of the couch which everybody took turns using, phone books on laps and constant questioning of how to access an outside line.

"First came the phone call for us. The time indicated the surgery had been on the short side, which I hoped indicated it had gone well. I don't remember the order of doctors coming or even what they said. I do know that when the phone call came, they indicated that it had gone well and altogether, I think we were in the room for roughly five hours, including the wait for the various doctors."

PROGRESS NOTES
11/22 13:00 Admission Anne Dusault, RN

Received to RR with Dr. Raudzens present. Pt. intubated. ET taped at 24cm oral airway present . . . good air exchange, diminished breath sounds on ausc . . . Dr. Raudzens informed, medicated with Procardia 10mg SL per Dr. Morcos for systolic s170. Pt. unresponsive to verbal/physical stimuli.

This was on Tuesday, the twenty-second. I did not move a muscle until late in the afternoon of the twenty-third.

11/23 00:00 Assessment Shift Anita Wright, RN, BNI
EP #3 Pt. awake, alert and oriented X4. Offering conversation and talking about his family . . .

At which time the famous surgeon Spetzler walked in and looked at me. He asked me my name.

"J.B. Number 1," I said.

He asked me what city I was in.

"Topeka," I said.

When they told my wife, who was outside, she said, "So far so good. He was like that when he came here."

I vaguely remember something like that. I guess I had a couple of smart remarks stored in my tongue so I could show off by reflex through the haze. Then I dropped in and out as I would for the next couple of days.

I woke up with a start and immediately

tried to throw my legs off the side of the bed and get up.

"You cannot move, you just had surgery," a woman said. She was a dim form somewhere near the bed.

"Is it over?" I said.

"Yes, of course. You had it yesterday morning."

"How did it go?"

"It's fine. You are fine. Don't worry."

I remember a thought running in an arc. I owed God thanks and I would have to be thankful for the rest of my life and I knew exactly how I was going to show it, but the arc never touched anything else and it disappeared and I didn't know what I was thinking about.

This was late in the afternoon of Wednesday, November 23. I was in Intensive Care. A titanium clip had replaced the aneurysm that could have figured in my vital statistics.

In Intensive Care, the nurses were Sharon Schwartz from Phoenix, in her sixth year here, and Mary King, who was from Wisconsin, and has been here for eleven years. Two weeks before, they had a young woman in room four who came out of a long surgery for a ruptured aneurysm. She rebelled before the nurses had all her lines and tubes connected and she had to go back to surgery. They also had a "numbers man" roll in from surgery. "Get me five," he said when he woke up. He was asked how he felt. "Five."

Mary King's husband, a machinist, doesn't like to come to the hospital to meet her and on the few times that she lured him upstairs to pick her up at her desk, he wouldn't look. He was in and out.

The computer printouts for this time are the symbols for the hours:

10:06. MD visit. Dr. Miller at bedside. Confirmed need to deep breathe with pt.

10:25. MD visit. Dr. Spetzler at bedside, answered pt's and family's questions about surgery and discharge.

18:00. Admission. Claire Lohan RN. Spoke one to two words, prefers to use motion of head rather than speech/opened eyes to command for brief second/ moves / moves independently. Very drowsy.

11:00. Introduced himself to nurse on this shift. Nursing routines explained prior and during implemention and verbalized understanding.

I kept seeing the Morgan Library. It's on Madison Avenue in the 30s. A rich white stone building. Then I knew why I was seeing it. They told me the Morgan would have a record of who owned the big Rubens painting from Lady Cynthia's living room. I could see her for a moment, standing by the painting. She had to be dead a long time. I'm walking to the Morgan Library to inquire if they could look up the painting's present owner for me. The white building on the corner, there is all this barbed wire in the way. The sun shining on it making it even uglier. Coils of barbed wire all over the place.

It was a long time later, I had been asleep I imagine, when I thought of the Morgan Library again, and this time I knew why the barbed wire had been there. It was the start of winter, and for the Christmas season they had barbed wire over the steam grates on the Madison Avenue side of the building. Don't let the bums get warm on Christmas Eve. Give them a real present. Hypothermia. I call them bums because I hate the word homeless. I hear homeless I see a cocktail party for the homeless. And now I have a vague exhilaration as I come up with the second thought. The day I was at the Morgan Library, a photographer from the paper came up to me and said I better get down in the subway right now, a white guy just shot four black kids on the Broadway line. The white guy jumped off the train and disappeared. So instead of looking up who owned a painting, I went into the subway and they had four kids shot pretty good. One of them is in a wheelchair forever, right now. This was the case of Bernhard Goetz. He had curled on a seat like a caterpillar and waited there, with a gun in his belt, for somebody to try and rob him and of course these four young morons went right for him and that was all there was to that. Goetz shot them and kept shooting. One of them went down and he stood over the kid and put another shot into him. A true hero. The bullets ricocheted all over the place. He was such a great public hero he could've killed women with shopping bags.

What am I thinking of this for? I started out reaching for something lovely, that painting again, and I wind up going through barbed wire to the ugliness of Goetz.

I don't know when it was, before dawn or just at dusk, but I began to congratulate myself on love. I was alive and in love. It is wondrous, fascinating, voluntary and occurs on the breathing of a crystal of air. You do not fall in love upon reflection. It is so much easier and so far more powerful than a friendship with men. To begin with, you can have a hundred friends but there is no way that you can live without a woman. What are you supposed to do, live alone? Friends are fine, but at all times, lurking beneath the glad smiles, is the fervent hope that the friend should fail at whatever it is he is doing. That I should succeed is great. But that my friend should fail! Fail so miserably that his face is covered with wet gratitude when he sees your hand extended in friendship and assistance. Real close friends are like fight trainers who crouch on the top step to the ring and cannot wait to swing through the ropes and pick your body off the floor. I think that the male who knows a little bit about himself finds no such bitter emotion in a marriage. If the woman can succeed at a career, then he, too, succeeds. Only a poor fool is jealous. The guy also better understand the strength of women and their disdain for men. I can see right now Fifth Avenue in Brooklyn. The Verrazano Bridge rises over the three- and four-story buildings. On one side of the street, young women and their mothers are going into Kleinfeld's, the most famous wedding gown store in New York. They spend thousands, two thousand is nothing, on a dress. The guys waiting for them go directly across the street to Zeller's Tuxedo Rental where they rent a tuxedo for the wedding day for

$88. If they bring the whole party of ushers and best man, they get the tuxedo thrown in for nothing, and that is exactly what the guy is worth at a wedding. From that day on, he better concentrate on his immense luck. The idea that a woman actually would live with you! Look at this. I was alive and I was in love. Sometime, when I can sit with a clear head and calm emotions, I am going to reason why I have been given such a marvelous break by God.

Right away, I felt this rush of air. A car only feet away from me and I never feel it hitting me. Or I am walking along and I hear the start of a shout and nothing else as an iron pipe falling from construction thirty stories up goes through my head. Some horrible fate someplace. I deserve it.

And now look at this, look at what happens when I try to have a decent thought. Right away, because I dared think love, I start asking myself how many wives Klein the Lawyer had. Three or four? I tried to put them into sequence. But when I looked, one of them floated into fog. Another had her back turned to me. When she turned around, she was not there. The next time I thought of this it was dark. Why am I thinking of Klein at this time? I had to get up and catch the train because I was supposed to go to the wedding today. I was still having trouble. I would see one wife, then another. I could hear Klein telling me that he was going to get married for the fourth time and I didn't see his third marriage in my mind.

They had a Super Bowl game on in the Part One bar and they told Klein it was the city high school championship game and that was good enough for him.

Now into the bar came a woman who looked exactly like Klein's first wife, who was at home. This new woman had the same dark hair and slightly protruding teeth that his wife had, and that is why he instantly fell in love with her.

He threw a bankroll on the bar to look rich. It included Debbie the secretary's salary.

When he told her it was the high school championship, she said, "Oh, is John Adams High School playing them? My girlfriend Helma Hartog was a cheerleader for John Adams. She lives down the hall from me. She's very unhappy. Her husband is a bologna slicer at a delicatessen. Helma Hartog wants him to do something better than that."

"What's he supposed to do?" Klein said.

"She wants him to be a gangster."

Klein took the hand of the new girl who

also had slightly protruding teeth.

And that was how he lost his first marriage. When this second wife said, "I want to borrow your car to go shopping," Klein went out and bought her a new Cadillac.

The marriage was good and her health was not. She died of cancer and Klein was there for her, and for her family. But I couldn't figure out anything past this.

I think of a library, I see barbed wire. I think of love, I get Klein. And I still could not believe that Klein the Lawyer brought Burton Pugash into his office just because he would do appeals at a cut rate. I remember when Burt went crazy over Linda. He was married and she told him, get out of here, she had a boyfriend who was going to give her a big ring. Burt went insane. He hired two guys to throw acid into Linda's face. Burt paid them only a couple of thousand. You get what you pay for. In this case, public speakers. They testified against him and he went to Attica Prison for fifteen years. I had to think for a moment. Do I have the money to get to the wedding? Had I known this last night, I would've had the money in my suit pocket right now. Leave without waking anybody up. I looked around for a closet. There wasn't even a closet in the room. I sure didn't know where

I was now. So I concentrated on remembering things about Burt Pugash. Every time he put in for parole, Linda went screaming to Burt Roberts, who was the Bronx district attorney then. She could see a little through big smoked glasses and she used to scream, "Pugash should die twice in jail." He got out when his time was up. He is walking along free on Queens Boulevard, and here was Linda, out for the air in smoked glasses. She says "Hello" to Burt Pugash. Can you believe this? She speaks to Burt Pugash. "Hello," she says. And Burt Pugash says to her, "I still love you." Linda says, "You do? That's nice." They went and got married. Now we have Burt in Klein's office writing appeals on the cases that Klein lost. Every Saturday, Burt is walking with Linda on his arm through the supermarket. She says what she wants and he picks it off the shelf. They are a very great love story.

"Don't get up!"

I'm getting up to make the wedding with them. It's a big wedding. I hate it. I don't want to go to it but I have to.

This time the nurse was more than a vague form. This time she had a hand on my chest. "You just had surgery and you cannot get up!"

Over the next couple of days, Dr. Peter

Raudzens, the head of neuroanesthesia, who put me to sleep, came by and when he caught me awake, I kept asking him to tell me something else about what they had done to me.

"I am not all that familiar with brain surgery," I said.

He answered, "Do you really want to know all this?"

The moment the operation was over and my head was taken out of these clamps that were holding it in the air, the barbiturates were stopped. Dr. Raudzens said the barbiturates have a half-life of twenty minutes to a half hour and I was then awake. Maybe someplace a record would show that, but I sure wasn't so terrifically alert or capable of motion except for moments like now, a day later or whatever it is, when I want so desperately to get out of bed and go to the wedding. I would write about it in the paper.

My head felt as rutted, as rough, as Queens Boulevard. I had a pain from the top of my head to my jaw.

"I need coffee," I said. I wanted to have coffee and then start working. I had a cup of coffee. Then I threw up. I knew it was going to be a while before I could try any work.

At first, I barely noticed hospital life. I

never knew until somebody mentioned it weeks later that I was at first in a room in Intensive Care with a woman. Had I known that, I would've crawled out. I take all my sickness alone.

But I did have my wife and two of her daughters and my daughter in Phoenix. During one night, I ran my first fever, 102°, and my daughter called one of her brothers in New York, who then made a lot of worried phone calls to doctors at Barrow. He came down on the next plane. Immediately, he was as nervous as everybody else. I had a heart monitor on my left side, a large needle in my right neck, with tubes sending in fluids, and in the middle of the night a 102° fever that everybody was afraid of.

The fever was from the small pneumonia I had. I guess that goes with the hospital bed. Jim Miller, the doctor, was around a lot now. It had nothing to do with my head, but the nurses kept putting lights into my eyes and the pupils constricted as they should. If the pupils dilate, somebody better reach for the emergency cord. He kept pressing on my calves to make sure there were no blood clots forming. He did ask me for my name and where I was. So did the nurses, day or night. They had to determine if I was oriented. Miller asked me again if

I drank. I told him no more. He shrugged. Ask Raudzens, I said. But even dazed in bed, I had saloon mannerisms. He would wait and see. The last guy who came in denied that he ever had had a drink in his whole life and on the third day in the hospital room he threw a colossal fit of the DT's and had to be restrained.

PROGRESS NOTES
0800 11/27
Pt. alert and oriented. Has bad H/A not better since AM med. Pt. is also nauseated and did not eat very much. Sat up in chair for ten minutes.
-0-

The close watch on me went that way for ten days. All notes are on a computer. Every room has a computer terminal on a table. At first it is part of the room, an extra vase for flowers. Then on each visit, a nurse or doctor taps an entry. They could call up my record practically to the minute, starting when I first walked into the hospital. Whenever I was half alert, and somebody would start on the machine, I would be torn with anxiety. I had to start work immediately on my newspaper job. I knew I had not written a column today, whatever day it was.

This was not fanaticism or wavering thoughts during a stupor. Since I started my newspaper column in 1962, I had not missed one deadline ever. I had a flu in 1968 and took three days off. But I never had started a column and not finished in time. And now the end of an afternoon caused instant anxiety; I had to be writing on edition time to pay for the rent.

I was raised on the story of Wally Pipp, a first baseman for the New York Yankees. One afternoon, Pipp told the manager, "I have a headache. I just don't feel like playing today."

The manager sighed. "I guess we're just going to have to go with this kid Gehrig."

The replacement, Lou Gehrig, went to first base and Pipp went home. He said he would be back and ready to play the next day.

Two thousand one hundred thirty games later, Lou Gehrig finally left the Yankee lineup. Pipp wasn't even a memory. That story keeps a lot of people I know from calling in sick with a common cold. But my concern now was not about a replacement. I was worried that something had happened to me in the operation. I noticed as I talked that I would slur, or even skip a word, or miss an entire part of a thought.

"I did better than this when I used to drink," I said.

I remembered that just before this started, I came out of a courthouse with Alan Futerfas, who plays the bass trombone in a brass quintet and defends Mafia gangsters. We were walking to his car and talking about keeping facts straight.

"All I have to do is use my memory," I said. "When I say something, I just don't say it. I speak ex cathedra."

"Do you remember the first time we met?" he said.

"At the bar in Joe Zito's. You just won with him in federal court."

Joe Zito owned a restaurant and had been charged with being a gangster. There were so many defendants that he wound up sitting next to me in the spectators' seats. "If they call my name, you stand up," Joe told me.

Futerfas asked me quietly, "What was I drinking the first time we met?"

I knew that. I could see us all standing at the bar. Joe Zito shouted that Futerfas was the new big lawyer for all decent gangsters. Futerfas held a glass and smiled. Good. I can see him there. Now what was in the glass? I tried to see the glass and smell what was in it.

"Vodka," I said.

He shook his head.

"Then it had to be Scotch and water," I said.

"I don't drink," he said. "It was soda."

He held the car door for me. Not only was I freaking embarrassed, but it left an uneasiness in me that never had been there before. My billion-dollar memory suddenly was shaky. That happened even before the prospects of having an operation. Of course the strength of the memory I was sure I had, and most times certainly did have, came from having to rely on it for a living so much. But what happens if doctors were in there with the pliers for too long? I'll wind up walking the beach in July in a thick black overcoat.

My wife, Ronnie Eldridge, reminded me that anesthesia had done that to her in an operation she had fifteen years ago. It was plausible but it didn't stop me from thinking about the loss of my full ability to do what I always did.

Then, with some exhilaration, I decided that it was only the third wife that went to visit Klein in prison. Or she was supposed to visit him. Klein's law partners gave her tickets to Florida. "How was he?" they asked her. She said, "I didn't see him this time.

I went to see my parents in Miami." The next ticket they gave her couldn't be changed. She had to fly straight to Panama City, the hometown of the jail. When she visited Klein at the correctional facility she said it was too hot and she wanted to return to the motel air conditioning.

And that is how, and now I figured it out, that Klein the Lawyer divorced his third wife and after that he married a fourth wife, who looked like the third wife, who looked like the second wife, who looked exactly like the first wife. And I never went to the wedding of the fourth wife because it happened a whole year before I ever got here to the hospital. Besides, Klein didn't want anybody to know he was this crazy, that he would get married four times, so I don't think anybody knew.

Now from nowhere, I heard Anthony Boscaino, who worked in the Cuomo grocery store, telling me how he knew he had the Sanitation Department job the moment he looked at the first question of the Civil Service test. The question asked the name of the president. Buscaino thought that was a natural question for a government job. He heard the guy at the next desk say, "Well, I got one right. The president of the United States is Fiorello LaGuardia."

"You mean you got one wrong," Buscaino said.

I could remember that nice. And this time, one thought led into another. I went swimming at John Jay College on Tenth Avenue and when I came home, my wife Ronnie Eldridge said, "Mario called. He read me his statement. He says he is running. Then, you know him, he said, 'But some of my people are still against this.' "

"But he said he was running," I remember saying.

"Yes, here. I even made some notes."

With that, she gave me the notes, put a "Cuomo for President" button on her coat and went out to work at City Hall. I called Fabian Palomino and asked him to have Mario send me an old-fashioned Western Union telegram, the kind on yellow paper they deliver by hand. "Just put down, 'I am running for president.' It would be good. I can leave it in the family."

Then at 1:00 P.M. he called me and said, "You might not get that telegram."

"What are you talking about? Tell him take thirty seconds and send the freaking thing."

"No, there might not be a telegram anywhere," Fabian said. "I don't think there is going to be anything to send about. The family is against this."

Cuomo called it off. The day displayed both his greatest strength and weakness. Perhaps he did not want to run because he thought it was not for him and was wise enough to know that this was a limitation that best be observed. But the fact that he didn't trust anybody enough to tell them about it is a great weakness and could have gone into deciding not to run. That was the thought I had here in bed. It was a great thought because it was a judgment. Good boy. That is what I do for a living. I write opinion. I get prizes for it and money for it. And it's also a lot of fun. All around me, I hear people say, "Oh, I'm nonjudgmental." Where did that come from? Is that a synonym for nonalive? What kind of venom can you raise, how much spite can you hurl out, if you limit yourself to deciding on nothing? If you are alive, you ought to enjoy an opinion on the president's girlfriends.

So I felt good about having an opinion. Now I went back to the Klein problem. He met a woman who looked exactly like his first wife and also exactly like the second wife. He wound up married again. This new wife, the third wife, held up a bare wrist. "Why don't I have something to wear like all my friends do?" she said.

He went to a thief he defended and bought a bracelet that was swag but still cost a fortune.

But that only makes three. I could not figure out the fourth.

Then at eight o'clock one morning, when the hospital room phones opened up, an old friend, Dick Donahue, called. He had been in the Kennedy White House and now he had just left the job of president of Nike with a hundred million dollars or so. He went from one topic to another at a swift pace and I kept up with him. He said that the Chinese would make products with a reduction of thirty-five to forty percent in the workers. He said that what we once called the Underclass soon will be an entirely different group. "We raised great file clerks and then we put a computer in an office and replaced clerks forever," he said.

In talking to him, my tongue missed a word here and there or slurred one. I didn't sense that he noticed this, but I thought that this was because I tried hard to cover all lapses.

Dick Donahue is from Lowell, Massachusetts. Right away, I knew that the writer Jack Kerouac came from Lowell. Then he lived on my block in Richmond Hill. His mother went to work in a factory every morning. Kerouac wrote fast and grim. Can't any of these people smile? I never got over reading that William Burroughs was from the Burroughs adding machine company and that he lived on a trust fund. A fake and a fraud. You, too, can be a great drug addict if your father leaves you the money to pay for the drugs. When Kerouac died in 1969, I went with his agent and a couple of people up to Lowell for the funeral. It was in the old French church at one end of Lowell. Afterward, we went to his frame house and I don't have my foot in the kitchen, looking for coffee or a drink, when it started. A relative said to Kerouac's agent:

"Boy, I'll bet there's plenty of good sales you can make with what Jackie left."

"What do you think could sell for the most?" somebody else said.

"That Jackie left a lot of real good stories you could sell," another said.

I remember waving good-bye to Allen Ginsberg and I went out the side door and into the early fall chill.

Here I am able to think of something and even to connect one thought to another. But is everything immediately going to be sour? Instead of numbers, my particular deficit will be to speak only with spite.

And none of this, even the depressing colors of anything I thought of, had much to do with writing. Thoughts flash and don't need order. Words seep, and must be put in alignments that are painful to write. I find anything from a postcard to a novel causes me to freeze from mind to hand. The effort to get a couple of sentences into the hand could take hours and hours. I had these streaks of thought, notion, the start of an idea of something to write. I looked for the dust in the air, for that is where words live, tumbling lazily, remaining just out of reach, and staying there, staying, staying, staying, until something, an unseen waft of air, causes them to drift right up to your reach, gather into sentences, one sentence, two sentences, that's all you need to get started. But now in this hospital room my eyes could find no dust.

I now was becoming apprehensive about my newspaper column. If anything had happened to the language center of the brain, I was through. For there is no way to learn how to write. I can do a column. You are born able to do something like a column or if not, you spend your life in a newspaper tortured by inability and never writing one sentence that anybody would remember.

I spent two days nervously trying to think

of a first sentence to start off a column. I picked up a pad and pen and with an effort that sapped me, I got a few paragraphs down. The next day I picked it up and wrote quite a bit. My wife went back to the hotel and typed it on a computer. When she showed it to me the next morning, she said nothing. I knew that she would wait for a chance to bring up objections, which her face showed would be at least many. She was right. My column read like pure Croatian.

I dropped my head in dejection. Then I told myself, if I knew it was lousy, then I still can think enough to do it right. I started writing again. The subject was the same one that you are reading about and I am writing. My brain operation. It took eight hours over a day and a half but I got the column done and I knew it was all right. I held the legal pad out in front of me and I dialed the newspaper transcribing room. Suddenly, as I was dictating to the newspaper, I noticed that I missed no words and slurred none. I hung up with exhilaration running through me. Once, this moment would have sent me tearing across a street at early evening and bursting through the saloon doors and saying to myself, "You deserve a drink. You are a good person."

Here in the hospital I put my head back and waited for somebody to come in and say I could go home. There was nothing else. The game was simple and grotesque. If you are one of the few whose aneurysm is found before it ruptures, there isn't even an aspirin needed once your brain is the same and you leave the hospital. You might drop by in five years if you feel like it. But if it bursts before it is found, the person probably won't be writing any books about it.

PROGRESS NOTES:
12/1
Pt. presents as very stable without change from my assessment and care of him 18 hours ago. He is off the monitor basically refusing to be for the night. PROBLEMS LIST: #1 He presents as being extraordinarily well versed on his condition and says there is no longer need for my attention.
12/1 12:30. No change in assessment. Discharge instructions given Pt. and family.
Discharged with wife to hotel.
-0-

The room in the Arizona Biltmore was on the ground floor and we opened the doors to a lawn and terrace. A large fountain was right outside. The room became filled with the sound of water running over rocks. I could hear it, I knew what it was and I could describe it in words. I had everything I ever needed to work for a living back in the same condition it always was. I sure have my remembrances of things in the past that are painful, but I have them. I remember pretty much everything. And as long as I can remember, I can be free. I have everything back, everything as it was. Beautiful.

Suddenly, I decided that the entire journey, this dangerous operation on the only brain I have, turned out pretty well. I want to thank God for letting me live, and I want to thank my brain for remembering me. Good boy yourself, Breslin. You rate a miracle now and then.

The employees of Thorndike Press hope you have enjoyed this Large Print book. All our Large Print titles are designed for easy reading, and all our books are made to last. Other Thorndike Press Large Print books are available at your library, through selected bookstores, or directly from us.

For information about titles, please call:

(800) 223-2336

To share your comments, please write:

Publisher
Thorndike Press
P.O. Box 159
Thorndike, Maine 04986